ANTHROPOLOGY

ERIC R. WOLF
**DISTINGUISHED PROFESSOR OF ANTHROPOLOGY
HERBERT H. LEHMAN COLLEGE OF THE CITY UNIVERSITY
OF NEW YORK**

"Man be my metaphor"
—DYLAN THOMAS

W · W · Norton & Company · Inc · New York

*I owe thanks to many friends and students
who attended the incubation of this essay.
I am specially grateful to Frederick Wyatt
and Claude Conyers who assisted in its birth.*

Wolf, Eric Robert, 1923–
    Anthropology

    Reprint of the ed. published by Prentice-Hall,
Englewood Cliffs, N. J., in series: The Princeton
studies: humanistic scholarship in America.
      Bibliography: p.
      1. Anthropology.   I.   Series: The Princeton
studies: humanistic scholarship in America.
[GN24.W63 1974]   301.2   74–2372
ISBN 0-393-09290-9

Printed in the United States of America

1 2 3 4 5 6 7 8 9 0

ANTHROPOLOGY

FOREWORD

What is the purpose of humanistic scholarship? What, in fact, does the humanist scholar do?

The job of the humanist scholar is to organize our huge inheritance of culture, to make the past available to the present, to make the whole of civilization available to men who necessarily live in one small corner for one little stretch of time, and finally to judge, as a critic, the actions of the present by the experience of the past.

The humanist's task is to clear away the obstacles to our understanding of the past, to make our whole cultural heritage—primitive, pre-Columbian, African, Asian, aboriginal, Near Eastern, classical, medieval, European, American, contemporary, and all the rest—accessible to us. He must sift the whole of man's culture again and again, reassessing, reinterpreting, rediscovering, translating into a modern idiom, making available the materials and the blueprints with which his contemporaries can build their own culture, bringing to the center of the stage that which a past generation has judged irrelevant but which is now again usable, sending into storage that which has become, for the moment, too familiar and too habitual to stir our imagination, preserving it for a posterity to which it will once more seem fresh.

The humanist does all this by the exercise of exact scholarship. He must have the erudition of the historian, the critical abilities of the philosopher, the objectivity of the scientist, and the imagination of all three. The scholar who studies the history of science, for example, must combine a knowledge of languages, history, and philosophy with the knowledge of a scientist. And so on with the scholars who study music, art, religion, literature, and all the rest.

The job is, obviously, impossible for any man; and the humanist scholar, knowing he can never attain his true goal, is always tempted to run after wooden idols whose cults are less exacting and which proffer an easy bliss.

Sometimes the humanist is tempted to bypass the rigorous training of the scholar and to wrap himself in the cloak of the sophist. Then he lapses into a painful wooliness and becomes the "literary" sort of humanist whose only accomplishment is a style which achieves the appearance of sublimity at the cost of an actual inanity. His opposite number is the hard-headed humanist who reacts against empty loftiness by becoming a pedant: he devotes himself to antiquarian detail no less trivial than the banalities of some social science or the mere collecting spirit which is sometimes found in the natural sciences. "Physical science can be at least as trivial as any other form of industry: but this is less obvious to the outsider because the triviality is concealed in the decent obscurity of a learned language."

Given the magnitude of his task and the impossibility of total perfection, the humanist scholar must, of course, specialize and his works will often be esoteric. But the belief persists that somehow specialization must be converted to generalization if the humanist scholar is to complete his job. Humanist scholars have not solved the problems of excessive specialization and must share the blame for that catastrophe of communication which besets modern learning.

Humanist scholars have been accused of being overly gen-
teel, contemptuous of popular culture, snobbish and anti-
democratic after the fashion of their aristocratic Renaissance
progenitors, backward looking, hostile to the present, fearful
of the future, ignorantly petulant about science, technology,
and the Industrial Revolution—"natural Luddites." "It is a
sad thought indeed that our civilization has not produced a
New Vision," a modern technologist complains, "which could
guide us into the new 'Golden Age' which has now become
physically possible, but only physically. . . . Who is responsible for this tragi-comedy of Man frustrated by success? . . .
Who has left Mankind without a vision? The predictable
part of the future may be a job for electronic predictors but
the part of it which is not predictable, which is largely a matter of free human choice, is not the business of the machines,
nor of scientists . . . but it ought to be, as it was in the great
epochs of the past, the prerogative of the inspired humanists."
(Dennis Gabor, "Inventing the Future," *Encounter*, May
1960, p. 15.)

Scholars in the humanities may modestly reject the sug-
gestion that they can ever be the inspired prophets of a new
age. But their scholarship is essential to enable us to distinguish the inspired prophets from the fanatical Pied Pipers.

The Ford Humanities Project under the direction of the
Council of the Humanities of Princeton University is looking
at American humanistic scholarship of recent decades, describing it, and attempting to sift the imaginative, the original, and the admirable from the pedantic, the conventional,
and the superficial.

We have commissioned about a dozen volumes by recognized scholars in each field. These volumes will give us an

account of American humanistic scholarship enabling us to see just what that scholarship has contributed to the culture of America and the world.

The decision to include a volume on anthropology in our series sprang from our somewhat vague feeling that this discipline raised fundamental questions about the relation of the sciences and the humanities and that anthropology itself was concerned about its humanistic bearings. Professor Wolf's essay proves that our vague feeling was founded on solid fact.

In demonstrating that anthropology is "the most scientific of the humanities [and] the most humanist of the sciences," Professor Wolf does more: he demonstrates that all science, in its dependence upon imagination and in its search for answers which are meaningful to men, is fundamentally humanistic and that the popular game of defining "two cultures" is sterile. But it is true, perhaps, that anthropologists are more conscious than other scientific investigators that "we shall never have completely open minds; it is likely that we should not want them. Only computers have completely open minds, and they must be put to work by minds that know what they want."

Finally, Professor Wolf shows how scientific investigation, imaginatively pursued, ends in a quasi-religious vision of the human predicament and the human future. The anthropologist draws from his discipline a rational faith which sustains his work and gives him his goal. Has any humanistic discipline ever done more?

RICHARD SCHLATTER
General Editor

INTRODUCTION

The essay which lies before you was written some ten years ago, and took a decade to graduate from an expensive hardcover edition of restricted distribution to the more accessible format of the paperback. Its subject matter is anthropology, but it is neither a history of that discipline nor a review of traditional anthropological subject matter. Instead, it attempts to look at the ways in which anthropologists in the United States have approached and interpreted that subject matter during the years following upon World War II. In brief, it says that the anthropological mode of cognition in America in the years between 1946 and 1964 was marked by three related tendencies: (1) a tendency away from a humanistically oriented concept of culture and toward a greater reliance on "society," thought of as an apparatus for the solution of human problems, with "culture" interpreted as the code for the operations of that apparatus; (2) a shift from a view of the culturally constituted personality as a bearer of common values to a model of an "organization man," ready to be slotted into the problem-solving societal machinery; and (3) a movement away from an interest in the uniqueness and diversity of cultures and toward an interest in the evolution of ever larger and more encompassing social and cultural systems.

The book sought some of the reasons for these shifts in the larger social and cultural environment within which American anthropologists carried on their work and earned their living. Implicit in such an approach is the premise that knowledge is not built up "after the fact," but in the course of socially and culturally conditioned interaction between material and men. American anthropology appears in these pages as the cultural outcome of a set of activities carried on by anthropologists, a specifiable group working in historic time and space and within identifiable social coordinates and cultural parameters. Among the possibilities suggested by this book, then, is the possibility of a sociology of anthropological knowledge.

When it was written ten years ago, this essay also had a second aim: to stress the distinctive interdisciplinary role of American anthropology. In contrast to the anthropological traditions of other countries, anthropology in the United States always prided itself upon its role as the unified and unifying study of several subdisciplines. In combining the pursuits of human biology, linguistics, prehistory, and ethnology, American anthropology put a premium upon intellectual synthesis, upon the tracing out of connections where others saw only divergence. Thus American anthropology grew up as a discipline between disciplines, and not merely as a discipline in its own right. I think that this has been one of its glories, and the source of its distinctive contributions. Yet this distinctive role is ever under challenge, as investigators stake out delimited territories within the larger discipline. Such specialization often has methodological justification, but may lose in theoretical import what it gains by narrowing its focus of attention. The essay thus expressed the hope that American anthropologists would not forsake their past, but continue the effort to construct an integrated and integral Science of Man.

A decade ago, such an integral science seemed not only possible, but imminent. The growing convergence of anthropological approaches and the considerable productivity of anthropologists appeared to presage such integration. This expectation has not been realized during the past decade. The reasons for this, as for previous trends, lie in the social and cultural context of anthropology in the United States. While in the years after the Second World War American society seemed to have achieved a stable and dynamic equilibrium, in the early sixties its social and cultural order began to exhibit signs of increasing strain. Rising dissension at home and escalating war abroad revealed abiding contradictions, deeply unsettling for a society which had always lived in the expectation that "tomorrow was another day," in which the future could continuously be created anew. Suddenly an unrequited past—a past of Indian wars, slavery, of colonial and neo-colonial expansion—rose up to plague the living. A host of forgotten victims and dissenters from the American Dream pressed demands which dispelled the easy-going assumptions of a universal societal consensus. It became clear that Americans were linked to one another not only by tacit agreements to "split the difference," but by feuds and hatreds of long standing for which no wergild had as yet been paid. At the same time, in the fiery light cast by burning villages and towns in Southeast Asia, the American past and present seemed no longer so privileged, so singular, so splendid in isolation. It was—like the pasts of other populations—encumbered with the history of deeds done and left undone in hot and cold wars, in other places and at other times. It was, moreover, a past *shared* with others, *shared in* by others.

Such an experience could not but throw some doubt upon our views of culture and society, upon the assumptions and methods which American anthropology had elaborated during the period of its self-assured growth after World War II. Crises are always revelatory in that they bring to light aspects of reality hitherto repressed or left unacknowledged. Much of what was thought and done in American anthropology during that period now seems like a reflex of a falsely confident movement of American society towards global hegemony, of an onward march towards "modernization" on the American model, in disregard of the historical context which underwrote that hegemony and of all the unrequited pasts which would rise up to challenge its progression. Anthropological concepts, useful in their time and for other purposes, now fail to encompass the material thrown up by changing circumstances. This is perhaps most evident in the case of our inherited postulate of functional integration: the notion which abstracts a particular culture from its setting and then treats it as a quasi organism—as a singular, separate, highly bounded, self-maintaining and self-correcting system. In fact, the units of our study never were singular, highly bounded, and self-corrective. When some Hidatsa Indians broke off from the main tribe to form the Crow, Plains Indians had already become agents of the advancing fur trade. When anthropologists went out to study Africa, the populations of the continent had already changed in response to shifts in trade routes across the Sahara and the Indian Ocean, as well as to the impact of the transatlantic traffic in slaves. The expansion of Atlantic civilization long ago undermined the singularity and separateness of the world's population, as it undermined our own singularity. The tribes and peasants of the world are not so many independent cases, but nodes in a network of relations; and this network includes ourselves.

Much of the last ten years has been marked by the uncertainty produced by this realization. Some of the resulting confusion has been destructive, some of it will prove to be creative: at any rate, there is much work to be done. Having long seen cultures and societies as isolated and distinctive, we must learn to see them in interchange and cultural synthesis. Having learned to visualize cultural boundaries as fixed and stationary, we must now learn to see them as shifting and evanescent. We have stressed order, equilibrium, negative feedback; now we must come to terms with opposition, contradiction, conflict, rebellion, and revolution. We have laid great stress upon the human capacity to adapt; now we need to emphasize as well their considerable capacity to create. Human beings are not merely "broken upon the wheel of culture," to serve lifetime sentences at forced labor in meeting the functional prerequisites of their cultures. They also seek the Golden Fleece, and wrest the gift of fire from the Olympian gods. We have learned a good deal; but there is still more to learn—and to learn it, we must first rethink the categories of our thought and practice.

DECEMBER, 1973   E.R.W.
LONDON, ENGLAND

CONTENTS

THE NEW ANTHROPOLOGY

The purpose of this essay is to define and appraise the relationships between anthropology and the humanities in these United States over the period of the last twenty-five years. The question enshrines a dichotomy that may lead us to see anthropologists firmly ranged on one side, and the protagonists of the humanities on the other. This dichotomy is real to the extent that, in American academic life, anthropologists and disciples of the humanities find themselves organized into different academic departments, drawing upon different sources for financial support. Anthropology can receive funds from a national science foundation; anthropologists can be members of a scientific honorary society like Sigma Xi. They can, furthermore—and when convenient—wrap themselves in the mantle of science, and claim access to the superior *mana* of the hard sciences, while the practitioners of the humanities must confront the rigors of academia without the benefits of warmth drawn from the halo-effect of science and without the support of a national humanities foundation.

On the intellectual plane, however, the division is not nearly so obvious and clear-cut. Alfred L. Kroeber, long the *Altmeister* of American anthropology, found no difficulty in calling himself "one-half humanist." Ruth Benedict, the author of *Patterns of Culture,* in her presidential address to the American Anthropological Association in 1948, gave voice to the conviction that "today the scientific and humanist tradi-

tions are not opposites nor mutually exclusive. They are sup-
plementary." Robert Redfield predicted in 1953 that "in the
future the interests which anthropology shares with humanistic learning are likely to deepen and to become more fully
recognized." And Robert Spencer, a year later, even argued
that "in the last analysis, those cultural anthropologists who
have been most successful have been less the scientist and
more the humanist."

On the other hand, the humanities are not what they were,
for the Chinese wall that once surrounded the domain of pure
spirit has been breached—irrevocably—by irreverent barbar-
ians from the provinces of science and beyond. The "old" history long ago gave way to a "new" history, seriously concerned
with developments in its borderlands that it might turn to its
own advantage. An "old-style" literary criticism, bent on historical scholarship and intent on evaluation, has given way to
a "new" or "scientific" or "modern" criticism, attempting to
gain insight into the structural and functional properties of
literature through the organized use of nonliterary techniques
and bodies of knowledge. Modern classical studies, such as
Moses Finley's *The World of Odysseus* (1954) and E. R.
Dodds's *The Greeks and the Irrational* (1951), bear the im-
print of recent anthropological thinking and research, while
philosophers as diverse as Charles Morris, F. R. C. Northrop,
James Feibelman, and John Ladd have sought to come to
terms with the new possibilities suggested by anthropological
studies. In a recent paper, Abraham Edel even discerned the
inklings of a "new" philosophy, aiming at drawing up a
"moral map of the world, as one might be asked to draw a
linguistic or religious map." And, should some of the thoughts
of André Malraux, scattered throughout the pages of his *The*

Voices of Silence, take root on this side of the Atlantic, we may well witness the development of a transcultural approach to art that could be as congenial to the wandering anthropologist as a transcultural approach to literature or to history or to philosophy.

This essay, then, will be intent on describing and analyzing some of the ways in which these bodies of knowledge interpenetrate, rather than on refining an all too obvious polarity. It must restrict itself, in space and time, to America in the last quarter century. This, too, is an artificial division, set up only to be transcended. It would hardly be possible to talk intelligibly about American anthropology without mentioning the continuous stream of influences and irritations of the professional organism that have come to us from abroad. Certainly America developed a great indigenous fieldworker and theorist of evolution in Lewis Henry Morgan (1818-81), the Rochester lawyer, who in his *Ancient Society* (1877) had depicted the march of culture as a progressive development through successive stages from a state of savagery through barbarism to civilization. Yet, evolutionist thinking in America was sharply challenged by Franz Boas (1858-1943) who came to these shores from Germany, already a mature scholar, to set up the first teaching department of anthropology in the United States at Columbia University in 1899. It was Boas who strongly influenced the growing discipline toward a natural historical approach in the investigation of custom. Deductive reasoning and generalization were to be set aside for painstaking induction from limited bodies of carefully controlled data. Under this stimulus, American anthropologists were for a generation to turn their back on the attempt to formulate general laws of cultural development and to emphasize the collection and interpretation of cultural details, localized in both space and time. Until the advent of World War II, Columbia University, where Boas taught until his death, and the University of California at Berkeley, staffed by two students of Boas, Alfred L. Kroeber (1876-1960) and Robert H. Lowie (1883-1957), were to be the citadels of the particularizing positivistic approach disseminated by Boas. Harvard University, though maintaining a brahmin isolation from the Boas group, which had its social and intellectual roots in the Old World, merely echoed the Boasian point of view.

Similarly, American anthropology would have been much the poorer had it not been for the transatlantic influence of Alfred R. Radcliffe-Brown (1881-1955) and Bronislaw Malinowski (1884-1942). Both men, whose intellectual base was in England, were in revolt against a particularism that would divide the living organism of a culture into small separate bits, in order to trace their distribution over space and time. In place of the enumeration of customs and the attempt to create a "conjectural" history based on the comparison of inventories of custom derived from neighboring tribes, they wished to see life as lived in a society as a coherent whole, a system. To Malinowski the leading question was how the body of custom in a society functioned to satisfy human physical and psychological needs, a question that he attempted to answer in a series of magnificent monographs on the Trobriand Islanders of eastern New Guinea, starting with a description and analysis of their trade in his *Argonauts of the Western Pacific* (1922). To Radcliffe-Brown, the central question was the problem of social order, the maintenance of solidarity in the social body, a focus that lent cohesion to his

4

major field report on *The Andaman Islanders* (1922). Both men were concerned not with isolated customs, but with what they called the "functions" of customs, their contribution—in Malinowski's terms—to physical and psychological maintenance, or—in Radcliffe-Brown's approach—to the promotion of social orderliness.

Of the two, it was Radcliffe-Brown whose influence both here and abroad had proved to be the more enduring. Malinowski inspired in his students primarily a passion for careful and empathetic fieldwork, and this he transmitted to American students during his stay at Yale University between 1939 and 1942. He could fascinate both students and readers with his skill in tracing through the web of relationships within a single culture. Yet his approach did not lend itself to the systematic comparison of a number of cultures. Since he saw each culture as a scheme designed to answer universal needs, he could explain them only in terms of universal characteristics. Radcliffe-Brown's approach, however, resulted in a comparative anatomy of societies, in which social arrangements in different societies were compared systematically with one another. Incomparably the poorer fieldworker, he proved to be the more powerful theorist. His crystallized views, presented in a faculty seminar at the University of Chicago in 1937 and published as *A Natural Science of Society,* made an abiding impression. The focal point of Radcliffe-Brownian functionalism in the United States has been the University of Chicago where the English anthropologist taught between 1931 and 1937.

More recently, American anthropology has experienced another transatlantic influence in the repercussions set up by the work of Claude Lévi-Strauss in France. Lévi-Strauss, a guest in the United States from 1941 through 1947, is now a professor of anthropology at the Collège de France in Paris. Building upon the insights of the French scholar Marcel Mauss (1872-1950), he has been instrumental in introducing a new approach to the study of kinship, which sees social groups in systematic communication with one another through the exchange of wives, much as mechanical transmitters and receivers send and receive messages, or persons and groups receive and return economic goods. This approach has been elaborated in his *Les Structures élémentaires de la parenté* (1949). Similarly, Lévi-Strauss has given new impetus to the study of cognitive systems through the application of methods derived from the analysis of linguistic structures to the understanding of conceptual categories found in various primitive cultures. His influence will be materially increased through the recent translation into English of his works on *Anthropologie structurale* (1958) and *Le Totémisme aujourd'hui* (1962). Thus we may argue, without straining the facts unduly, that American anthropology owes the greater part of its theoretical armament to importations from across the Atlantic, which it has applied with its characteristic pragmatism to data collected by indigenous practitioners. One may note wryly that, for a long period of time, Lewis H. Morgan, the major American theorist, was a prophet everywhere but in his own country.

My imposed limitation in terms of time, the past twenty-five years, is more congenial, for the experience of World War II certainly altered both the social organization and the intellectual materials of the anthropological profession in the United States. Many of the trends toward change were already

6

under way before the war; but most of them showed a qualitative change, as well as a quantitative increment, after it.

The decade before the war had already witnessed a first expansion of American anthropologists into world areas outside of North America. The best known of these efforts are perhaps Margaret Mead's investigations in Samoa (1925-26) and New Guinea (1928, 1931-33); Robert Redfield's work in the Mexican village of Tepoztlán (1926-27) and later in Yucatan and Guatemala (in the 1930's); and John F. Embree's application of the community study method to a complex society in his study of Suye Mura in Japan (1935-36). There were, of course, others. But most American anthropologists still worked mainly or exclusively with American Indian groups, conveniently located in their own backyards, and strove, with varying success, to wring the last gasp of a dying culture from the lips of a moribund informant. New anthropologists were still trained to remember and analyze stock examples drawn from the fragmented and imperiled lifeways of Sioux or Navaho, drawing a bitter dole on ill-managed reservations.

The war changed all this radically. Numerous anthropologists went out to the Pacific, in the wake of occupying American forces, to assist the military governors installed in the many, culturally distinct, islands. Others labored in Washington or at their respective universities in the analysis of cultures then of strategic importance to the war effort of the United States. One such endeavor resulted in Ruth Benedict's elegant and controversial *The Chrysanthemum and the Sword* (1946), a study of Japan made without benefit of direct fieldwork in the country and wholly dependent on secondary materials. Another precipitate of the war years was the *Handbook of South American Indians,* edited by Julian H. Steward of the Smithsonian Institution, a work important both as a compendium of available knowledge on the Indian inhabitants of our sister continent to the south, and as an inspiration for new theoretical and practical inquiries after the war. With the end of hostilities, and the increasing sponsorship of investigations abroad by great public and private foundations in the postwar period, American anthropologists have since invaded in force all the major areas of the world not closed to them by hostile powers. At the same time, a new generation of American anthropologists is cutting its intellectual eye teeth on material drawn from the living societies of Asia, Africa, and Oceania, until the West African Tallensi and the societies of New Guinea have become as familiar in American anthropological discourse as the Hopi and Navaho Indians of the American Southwest.

At the same time, the war produced a heavy increase in the number of American anthropologists. Membership in the American Anthropological Association multiplied twenty fold in the period between 1941 and the present. The number of universities teaching anthropological subjects rose heavily, giving increased employment to professionals, while at the same time undermining the established monopolies of jobs and influence characteristic of the prewar period. The bullish behavior of the market for anthropologists brought on an increased occupational and geographical mobility, which threw together in many a department the disciples of quite different "schools" and produced intellectual cross currents that strongly reinforced already incipient American tendencies toward eclecticism. I shall be concerned with other side

8

effects in later discussions; but let it be clear that this essay concerns a demarcated period, even if its geographical limitations constitute a somewhat artificial restriction.

Whatever the temporal and spatial limits of the "present position" of American anthropology, its relation to other disciplines is clearly equivocal. The arguments advanced by both anthropologists and nonanthropologists regarding its precise location between the sciences and the humanities bespeak a significant degree of uncertainty. Where some would extend the intellectual boundaries of the anthropological enterprise to render nothing human alien to its efforts, others—favoring certainty and delineation—would restrict it to narrower and more measurable endeavors. Anthropology, as other disciplines, includes both imperialists who take their pleasure in swallowing up others and cultists who wish to manipulate their professionally sacred artifacts only within the inner precincts.

Yet there should be no denial of the fact that latter-day anthropology is an offspring—though marked by mutation —of "philosophical anthropology," the enterprise of the Enlightment aimed at understanding the inherent capabilities and limitations of man. This earlier anthropology casts its image of man in molds that have proved too narrow, whether they were Cartesian or Kantian, for the La Haye of Descartes and the Königsberg of Kant provided understandings of only one kind of men, the members of the articulate strata of European society. To arrive at a general definition of man, however, it was first necessary to examine the numerous varieties of men, and to decide whether they, too, were to be included within the limits of a definition of what it takes to be human. This need inevitably produced a new kind of anthropology that could include in the human account men till then not dreamed of in the repertoire of the philosophers. Indeed, latter-day anthropology has brought to fruition an undertaking begun by the Renaissance, which rediscovered the worlds of the Greeks and Romans and rendered these worlds contemporary in the process of rediscovery. Equally important was the European encounter with America, and its "natural" men. Next, the Orient took on reality and contemporaneity with the world of the West. Finally, anthropology turned its eyes upon the outcasts of civilization, the varied groups of primitives and peasants of the world, mute and inglorious inhabitants of its external margins.

Thus, in the past centuries, the inventory of humanity has come to include many "significant others"; the originally unified image of man has splintered into a thousand different, equally valid, refractions. The original query as to the nature of man and of the human enterprise remains; but with the increased heterogeneity of the material to be ordered and explained has come the need for a change in method. Anthropology furnishes that method in the naturalistic assessment of its multifarious material. This naturalism is a *sine qua non* of anthropology, an indispensable prerequisite also to new answers to the old question. The philosophers, the writers, the artists who first raised it felt that they could address themselves directly to the analysis of mind because they shared a common understanding of the matrix of common life in which this mind was set. Such common understanding rendered irrelevant the careful observation and recording of the material outlines of its daily toil. But the anthropologist who went out to consult the savages of the four corners of the earth could not concern himself with the improbable mental configurations of his subjects without making sense first of their unfamiliar physiques, their bizarre behavior, the strange objects they produced. He had to measure skulls, to collect things, to observe seemingly extravagant actions before he could ask reasonable questions regarding their mental concerns. The necessary techniques of the museum collector, the human biologist, and the field observer have made a naturalist of the anthropologist, whatever view he may hold regarding the primacy of mind over matter or of matter over mind.

This anthropological naturalism is, however, also *sui generis,* dualistic offspring of humanistic philosophy and science. Both humanist and anthropologist have shared a wish to escape from the reality that surrounds them; both have attempted transcendence. The humanist has attempted to rise above his world by abstracting the multiple visions of man from the matrix of the commonplace in which they are encased; and he has treated them as guideposts to the realm of the perfectible—the true, the good, and the beautiful—that is conceived to lie beyond the imperfect present. The anthropologist, too, has sought escape and transcendence. He has escaped from the humdrum world of his civilization to walk among headhunters, cannibals, and peyote-worshipers, to concern himself with talking drums, magic, and divine kings. Anthropology has thus shared in the wider characteristics of romanticism, but in that peculiar form of romanticism that, in Hoxie Fairchild's words, "arises from a desire to find the supernatural within the natural, or in other words, to achieve an emotionally satisfying fusion of the real and the unreal, the obvious and the mysterious." The anthropologist has shown a tendency, moreover, to construe these savage worlds as worlds *sui generis,* to hypostatize his Comechingon or Rame-kamekra into representatives of pristine designs for living, untouched by the hands of the civilization from which he escaped, where a more cynical and less romantic observer might see merely the castaways of civilization or the wreckage of cultures trampled under the feet of fur traders and black-birders. Where the humanist has often stressed what man might yet become, the anthropologist has pointed with delight to the nightside of human nature. One might say that anthro-pology is but a latter-day version of the descent into hell, into a strange and bizarre underworld, in which the hero—dis-guised as The Investigator—walks untouched among the shades because he carries in his hand the magic sword of Science. The humanist, on the other hand, is closer to the tradition of those seekers after perfection who have climbed the interior stairways of the soul toward some ulterior heaven.

If their common wish to transcend reality binds anthro-pologist and humanist together, more closely than they know, their means serve to divide them. In the study of the humani-ties, the subjective emotional component looms large. There are chastisements and disciplines of the soul, but the em-phasis is on the transcendence of what is, on creativity—or, at least, even in the biographical and critical exercise of the humble, on an identification with creativity. Anthropology, on the other hand, insists on the primacy of the real, in the guise of the apparently evil, the apparently false, the appar-ently ugly. It therefore insists on fieldwork, that form of ritual in which the investigator is tempered in the course of "partici-pant observation." Both have their virtues; both their vices. If the besetting vice of the humanities is an exaltation of in-herent subjectivity, the dominant vice of anthropology is a preoccupation with the easily demonstrable and the frequent relegation of insight to the realm of private conversation.

Thus anthropology is both a natural science, concerned with the organization and function of matter, and a humanistic discipline, concerned with the organization and function of mind. Its subject matter is man, who is both part of the ecology of nature and an improbable departure from what one might expect to find in the natural realm. He is the animal with culture, that is, an animal equipped with the ability to create and use symbols to devise new, artificial worlds of his own making. Just as the subject matter of anthropology is dual, so the concern of the anthropologist is dual: he must mediate between human biology and ecology on the one hand, between the study of human understanding on the other. Necessarily, he must be both outside observer and participant in the internal dialogues of his informants. By definition, therefore, anthropology is less subject matter than a bond between subject matters, and the anthropologist will forever find himself translating from one realm to another.

This task, however, also has historical dimensions. The conception of how the external and internal worlds are related to each other, as well as the manner of translation from one to the other, must needs change with changes in the social positions of both observer and observed. Five such major changes mark the postwar period that forms the temporal framework of this essay. I attribute these changes to two related shifts in viewpoint.

The first of these shifts occurred during the war years. World War II provided, for anthropologists as for others, a lesson in cultural dominance on a scale never seen before.

No one who witnessed the military buildup of the United States from a point of military unpreparedness where recruits still drilled with wooden rifles to the point of final assault on the redoubts built by the Axis powers could escape the realization that a great industrial society operated in terms of an energy potential very different from that commanded by a primitive society. Nor was there much chance to escape this experience of social mobilization. The lesson served not only the anthropologist, but also his informants. No native who saw the masses of men and material that passed through the Pacific on the way to Japan could be in doubt regarding the difference in scale, in level of output and complexity, between his own culture and that of the foreign armies. In one way or another, involvement in this war made obvious the size of the gap that separated the anthropologist and the primitive, while at the same time forging the bonds of a new relation. Where before the war the anthropologist had wished to approximate the native, as a result of the war the native wished to approximate the anthropologist. Where before the war the point of reference for the anthropologist had been the native culture, after the war the point of reference increasingly came to be his own culture.

The second shift in social viewpoint arose during the postwar years. Society, as a determinant, loomed not only larger in the military field; it loomed larger within its own boundaries. The war years and the postwar period saw the decline of many hopes that had staked their all on the capacity of men to reorder their own societies from the ground up. Society seemed more pervasive and all-embracing than before; the individual dwarfed by processes palpably beyond his personal control. David Riesman and his collaborators painted a picture of this shifting outlook in which the "inner-directed" man of the past, captain of his own soul, was giving way before the "other-directed," who steered his course not by his own compass, but in terms of the expectations of others. The faceless "other" acquired tyrannical shape, as the other-directed was cast in the role of the new "organization man." Whether or not this particular mutation is a reality—or, as the sociologist Bennett M. Berger has suggested, merely a nightmare of the intellectuals—the individual was caught up in a situation in which the complexities of life seemed beyond his span of control. He had to rely on others, to cooperate with others, to allow himself to receive instruction from others, in maintaining a process that, as a whole, appeared more powerful than himself. This shift also led to a feeling that, far from being able to remake the world, all one could do was to cultivate a tiny garden or—to use a more modern parlance—to retreat into a small shelter, not only unable to cope with society, but also abdicating one's responsibility to participate in it.

The first consequence of this last shift in attitude was a repression of the romantic motive in anthropology. Anthropologists have become more willing than they once were to call themselves social scientists, a term that for men like Alfred Kroeber still contains a note of opprobrium. In an article on the "History of Anthropological Thought" in the *Yearbook of Anthropology, 1955,* he wrote: "The older anthropology saw some broad problems and made generalizations. . . . But it contained also a strong sensory, aesthetic, and experiential interest. It liked artifacts, and it established museums; it was interested in the land and scenes in which people functioned; it liked to experience—at first vicariously and then in the flesh—how these people looked and behaved and what they had to say. It was part natural history in character, part humanities; but the humanities-like ingredient was non-normative, comparative, and broad ranging" (p. 307). But the new social science approach aims at constructing systems of general propositions. Facts are "marshalled towards an objective, like ranks of privates that are there to make Gen. Principle win a campaign" (p. 306) and—what is worse—"it is in such pale-gray depersonalized words that the findings are deliberately clothed. Life and color remain only in the quoted excerpts which humbly serve to validate the propositions that make the system" (pp. 306-07). Recently, William T. Jones has defined *The Romantic Syndrome* (1961) as a preference for the dynamic, the changing; for complexity, fluidity, and disorder over system, clarity, and structure; for participation in the inner experience of the objects of their study over a relatively external relation to them; for soft focus over sharply defined focus; for other-worldly bias, "a flight through time or a flight through space," over a this-worldly bias; all the very opposite of the Enlightenment syndrome. The contemporaneous dominance of the Enlightenment syndrome seems to be related to its significance for social engineering. What is wanted is predictability, standardization, problem solving.

There is yet another aspect of the anthropologist's romanticism that bears comment. I am referring here to the American anthropologist's preference for the term *culture* to cover the phenomena of his interest, as against the terms *society* and *civilization,* which are more to the taste of his British and French colleagues. This preference the Americans share with the Germans who have also made much of *Kultur.* In his book *Ueber den Prozess der Zivilisation* (1939), Norbert Elias has shown how this choice of different key terms is related to the different development of society in France and Germany during the seventeenth and eighteenth centuries.

In France, the growth of absolutism extended the sway of courtly forms over both aristocracy and the middle classes. "The courtly bourgeoisie and the courtly aristocracy both spoke the same language, read the same books, possessed—in regularly diminishing degree—the same manners, and when the growing disproportions in economy and society ruptured the institutional structure of the *ancien régime,* when the bourgeoisie became the nation, much of what was originally specifically courtly and differentiated the social character of the courtly aristocracy, and—later—of the courtly bourgeoisie, from that of other groups, suffered a transformation, expanding in ever growing intensity and in determined fashion into the national character: the manner of stylistic convention, the forms of behavior, the shaping of affect, the high value placed on politeness, the importance of good diction and conversation, the articulateness of speech, and more, all these—in France—are shaped originally within the society of the court, and develop in continuous expansion from a set of social characteristics into national ones" (vol. I, p. 44).

The process had parallels in England where, after the Reform Bill of 1832, the public schools were remodeled to make gentlemen of the great-grandsons of peasants and artisans whom social mobility had carried into the upper ranks of society. Leland Baldwin has pointed out in *God's Englishman* (1944) that the new model of behavior fused the aristocratic ideal of the gentleman with its "emphasis on ability to command, ease and dignity of deportment, an overwhelming feeling for style, and a certain tendency to obscure the deeper things of life under a veil of ritualism" with the Puritan ideal of man as a practitioner of "chastity and many of the other facets of self-control, such as devotion to duty and rigid mental and moral precepts" (p. 173). As in France, manners made men and cemented society.

Not so in Germany, where the middle classes had the opportunity neither to learn the manners of the court nor to grasp the reins of power. In France and England, the upper classes served as social reference groups for those below them; their manners were upheld as models of propriety. In Germany, however, there was no aristocracy with an indigenous courtly culture; the German aristocrats imported their manners and social ideals from France. Nor did the aristocracy take any part in the cultivation of German art and literature. These, too, were the products of the middle classes. Uncertain of their social position, politically atomized and deprived of power, the middle-class reaction in Germany took the form of an anti-French nationalism, directed both against foreign domination and against the francophile aristocracy. Characteristically, this nationalism reacted against foreign "mannerisms" and "foppery," and upheld the true-blue virtues of the native stock. These qualities, however, were said to reside not in outward show, but in "the inner man," that emphasis on internal moral worth that underlies also the concept of true—internal—culture. These internal qualities, as opposed to the veneer of social polish, have ever represented virtues to German social science, while civilization was regarded as mere outward show, mere exercise of technical skills. In American anthropology, the same polarity re-emerges, for example, in Alfred L. Kroeber's distinction between *value-culture* and *reality-culture,* and in Robert Redfield's employment of the terms *technical order* and *moral order.*

One may wish to speculate on this transfer of cultural baggage to the new and supposedly different world. In part it is no doubt due to the strong German influence on American academic life in general, especially before World War I. Nevertheless, there are also similarities in the social conditions of Germany and the United States that may have predisposed them to the common utilization of the culture concept. America, like Germany, disdains what it conceives to be artificiality and outer form; true being, here as there, is natural and is conceived to spring from the heart. On these shores, too, the sophisticated, hard, brilliant, unsentimental polish of manners—which creates social distance as much as it regulates social conduct—has been rejected in favor of an informality of manners that welcomes all comers. Frontier and melting pot discouraged "putting on airs"; men were to encounter men without the intervening barriers of polished forms. Perhaps, then, it was this stress on the informal and internal that made the German culture concept congenial to the Americans. To this day, American anthropologists still react with a sense of unreality to the analyses of their British colleagues, which bespeak a feeling for social fitness in role playing, for hierarchy and social balance, that does not square easily with the American experience. Nevertheless, here too we are witnessing a change. Perhaps as the American pattern crystallizes, we too find ourselves involved in changes that accentuate the social control of manners, and decrease shirt-sleeved informality. Correspondingly, how men *claim* to be is more important than what they *are;* the concept of society may yet gain over that of culture.

The second consequence of the postwar shift in outlook has been the retreat from the position that human nature was characterized by unlimited flexibility to a re-emphasis on the enduring features of the human psyche and sociality. Prewar anthropology had been concerned—nay, obsessed—with the discovery of human diversity. Ruth Benedict had given poetic voice to this concern in her *Patterns of Culture* (1934), in which she wrote of "the great arc" of human behavior, from which each culture selected only a limited number of possibilities. This thought she expressed beautifully in the image of the Californian Indian chief who spoke of a time when "God gave to every people a cup, a cup of clay, and from this cup they drank their life." There were as many cups as there were peoples; Benedict saw the common humanity of men precisely in their unlimited variability.

But where the anthropologists of the 1930's emphasized the free play of the human disposition, the anthropologists of the postwar period have returned to the question of cultural universals, to a renewed emphasis on the enduring features of the human psyche and sociality. Perhaps the temper of the 1930's—the temper of the New Deal and the Soviet "experiment"—favored the view that human nature was inherently flexible and, therefore, changeable. Perhaps the colder realities of the postwar world, which has seen the abortion or early demise of many a cherished utopia, have discouraged such optimism. The silhouette of the City of Man is seen in bleaker outlines against a colder sky. Human nature seems less malleable. It is the apparently inherent dilemmas of human existence that strike our consciousness, not the hope of their transcendence. If human nature has set limits, then it also appears changeable only within such limits. Periods of this kind render deliverance less tangible. They also set a mood in which men wish to escape from the relentless march of events they cannot control into a mythology that stresses the stable and the enduring. Men seek to define unchangeable archetypes, in the hope that behind the illusion of change they may discover a basic repetitive reality.

At the same time, this colder postwar world is a world of enormous societies pitted against each other, a world of dinosaurs in which the big lord it over the small, in which the facts of social and cultural dominance are inescapable. This dominance not only confronts the powerless and forces them to barter their freedom for safety; it also enshrines a large measure of unfreedom for the powerful, for those who possess dominance must wield it, and are thus caught up in the cares and responsibilities of power. There seems less room for change in the world; there are only possibilities for minor political maneuvers. Hence men feel oppressed by a double sense of limitation, the limitation of the field of action as much as the apparent limitation of the human material for action. This sense of limitation is at the roots of a new conservatism. If neither human nature nor society are really changeable, then our present society seems the best compromise solution possible, or, rather, the least of all possible evils. Anthropologists, no less than others, are responsive to such trends. Cultural relativism, inferred from the enormous variety of existing cultures, remains a prerequisite of objective analysis: one must first understand a culture in its own terms, not in terms of theoretical or practical schemes imposed on it from the outside. But the moral corollary of cultural relativism—moral relativism—has been quietly discarded, except as a form of intellectual indulgence among those who claim the privileges of noninvolvement.

The third consequence of the postwar shift has been the growing interest in the development of civilization, as opposed to the past interest in the cultures of primitives. Anthropology is thus returning to the society that it once abandoned. Studies of acculturation, of how primitives become members of modern society, together with studies of peasantries— groups of more or less tradition-bound populations *within* modern or modernizing society have come to the forefront. This change has two aspects. No longer are primitive cultures seen as pristine crystals existing in their own right, but as aspects related systematically to the on-going process of civilization. Thus, we are now asked to consider how the Iroquois or the Nootka became involved in the fur trade and the extent to which Iroquois and Nootka culture is explicable in terms of this involvement; how the Indians of the plains became a specialized subculture of the advancing colonial frontier, supplying the pioneers with meat and hides; how the Mexican Indian or the Pueblo village is not a culture *sui generis,* but a specific cultural structure developed in interaction with particular forces aiming at its disintegration. In considering the effects of acculturation the problem is no longer primarily the primitive outside the pale of civilization, but the persistent groups of tradition-bound populations within the gates, "the internal stranger." This trend, too, has reinforced the approximation with sociology that has hitherto concentrated on the study of our civilization. We are returning to ourselves, after fleeing from ourselves.

The fourth consequence of the postwar shift in point of

view, briefly mentioned in another context, has been the de-emphasis of cultural relativity. In the light of related factors, the concept is rapidly acquiring an old-fashioned ring. Not that the anthropologist has abandoned his attitudes of affective neutrality toward his subject matter; but with the decline of the romantic quest for pristine alternatives to our way of life we have abandoned also the superevaluation of primitivism that we have treasured hitherto. Especially in disrepute are arguments leading from cultural relativism to moral relativism, arguments that at all times have produced a great liberating effect from the tyranny of one's own customs, whether encountered in the works of the Marquis de Sade—one of the great cultural and moral relativists of all times—or in the vicarious thrill that accompanied the first reading of *Patterns of Culture* in the 1930's. Ruth Benedict herself pointed out that because human nature was variable enough to assume the different shapes of Hopi or Kwakiutl nature did not mean that American culture could be recast, using one or another feature of these cultures. But the concept of unlimited human variability, together with the sense that anything was possible and morally feasible, gave many people the feeling that their own lives could be recut upon some other pattern, that new and different possibilities were in the air. What is left of this attitude is the understanding that we must study each culture in its own terms. The attitude that here is another valued object, to be treasured for its very difference, a phenomenon that one may draw closer to oneself by investing it with affect, has given way to a colder neutrality, that of the engineer, for example, whose very way of knowing creates a distance between himself and the object investigated.

This change has also promoted and intensified the applied

or action aspect of anthropology, a development marked by the establishment in 1941 of a Society for Applied Anthropology, separate and apart from the American Anthropological Association. Applied anthropology, by definition, represents a reaction against cultural relativism, since it does not regard the culture that is applying anthropology as the equal of the culture to which anthropology is to be applied. At the present time, there indeed exists a division in the field between those who wish to use anthropology as a tool in social engineering, and those who want more mature theory, but not premature practice. This is not, however, a basic split, since there is a general sense in which indeed all anthropology is by nature applied anthropology.

The term may of course be construed narrowly to apply only to efforts to acquaint Mexican Indians with hybrid corn, to further the growth of public health in Ecuador, or to teach a group of reservation Indians to earn extra pennies by making pots and baskets for sale to eager tourists. Yet even such efforts quickly spill over into general theoretical considerations and public policy. Whether or not American Indians are to be allowed to use the narcotic peyote in the services of their Native American Church is in part a question of religious freedom in America, but in part also a theoretical question, involving consideration about integrative adjustments of people to conditions of cultural stress. Whether the Indian cultures of the United States are to be rooted out through forced acculturation or permitted to go their own way in cultural oases sheltered against encroachment by the law of the land is not only a question of justice, but also of feasibility, hence of anthropological theory. Yet one may well ask just what it is that the anthropologist brings to such efforts at application. Those who search the anthropological literature for "how-to-do-it" books will search in vain. For what the anthropologist contributes to these projects is not gadgetry, but the spirit of flexible inquiry. He takes his stand against petty ethnocentrisms, against the thoughtless and soulless application of principles and methods derived from one cultural setting to another, different one. If this is sometimes interpreted, in the idiom of cultural relativism, as "respect" before another culture, it is really no more than collective emotional maturity, a cognizance of possible obstacles, an unwillingness to barge into unfamiliar territory. By this act of hesitation, therefore, the anthropologist injects into the practical effort the criteria of his science, his sense that there are things not known beforehand, but to be found out. But what is science to some is timidity to others; and not all of his nonanthropological coworkers will heed the message. Hence, the successful application of anthropology is in part also a function of the process whereby people begin to learn and understand what anthropology is all about. Teaching anthropology is certainly also a form of applied anthropology.

The fifth consequence of the wartime shift, again related to the others, has been a major change of perspective on the role of personality in the maintenance of culture. Drawing in one way or another on the insights offered by psychoanalysis, prewar anthropology discussed individual personality primarily in the context of socialization. It looked to the study of socialization for the answers to the questions of how the individual was shaped to fit the demands of his culture and of how he passed cultural patterns on to his children. To the extent that each generation replicated the pattern handed on by its parents the culture would remain intact. A corollary of this was that each individual was in a sense a replica of the culture; he carried an image of the culture within him whose pattern resided in the emotions generated and organized during his childhood. The approach was contradictory, for while it turned the individual into the nearly faceless carrier of his culture—de-emphasizing his idiosyncratic development—it also made the individual responsible for cultural maintenance —responsible, hence important.

We now know this approach to have been too simple; it abstracted too much from the real differences between individuals that appear clearly in any test results applied to large populations. Yet, we must look to other factors besides empirical deficiency to explain the shift in emphasis—after all, the theory of evolution has come back into circulation among anthropologists, although none of the problems surrounding it have really been solved; there are simply more people now than there were in the 1920's willing to distinguish between simple and complex cultures and societies. For the shift in emphasis has greatly reduced stress on the organization of emotions in culture and vastly increased interest in the cognitive process. It is no longer held that all individuals in a culture must be emotionally tuned to the same wave length; it has become apparent, as Bert Kaplan has noted in his *Study of Rorschach Responses in Four Cultures* (1954), that "individuals seem a good deal more similar than they really are." That is, individuals play roles in society. It is not so important *what* they are; what is important is the extent to which they possess the necessary cognitions that allow them to play their roles adequately. Anthony Wallace has even stated his conviction that no individual need know all the cognitive elements of his culture; he need control only those that refer to his particular repertory of social roles. Patient and doctor, in our society, for instance, do not share the same cognitive elements; all that is necessary for a man to receive instructions from his doctor is for their cognitive elements to touch at certain strategic points. People may differ greatly, as long as they maintain a minimal conformity to certain cognitive expectations. (See Wallace's *Culture and Personality*, 1961.)

Where the old view relied on the individual to receive the elements of his culture and to pass them on to his children, as a relay runner hands on the staff to the next member of his squad, the new approach removes this responsibility from the individual. The organizing element in tradition is no longer within the individual; it is outside him, in society. The new man of the new anthropology is an "organization man" bending to the exigencies of his life situation. He is flexible in adapting to others and the requirements of others; indeed—in Wallace's view—he needs these others to complete him, since he carries within his own mind only a small part of the total cognitions necessary to sustain the social network. The locus for cultural maintenance has been shifted from the individual to the social system. The relay runner, handing his torch on to future generations, has become a cog in a depersonalized social machine.

The theoretical precipitates of these changes are manifold. I have already hinted at the renewed interest in evolution. This is itself remarkable, coming after a prolonged period of pronounced lack of interest in evolutionary perspectives and the outright antievolutionism of the prewar period. For many years, Leslie A. White was an evolutionist prophet crying in an antievolutionary wilderness that yielded no sympathetic echo. White had been a student of Boas at Columbia University, but had reacted strongly against the historical particularism of the Boas group. Teaching first at Buffalo and later at the University of Michigan, he had set himself the task of vindicating Morgan's position in American anthropology. In the immediate postwar period, his polemics with one of Boas' devoted followers, Robert H. Lowie of the University of California at Berkeley, set up profound repercussions in previously unsuspected ways. White's particular contribution to evolutionary studies—taking its departure from suggestions made by the German chemist Wilhelm Ostwald in "The Modern Theory of Energetics," written in 1907—made use of the concept of evolution as a process increasing the availability of per capita energy. But its greater general relevance lies in returning us to the original query of philosophical anthropology. For White again invites us to see the cultural process as a universal phenomenon, operating on a world basis—evolution is said to characterize world culture as a whole, not any particular individual culture. In 1774, the German philosopher Johann Herder had taken the then inevitable and necessary pragmatic step of particularizing the general history of man into the particular histories of this or that kind of man. White's universal view of culture, coming after the accumulation of particularistic knowledge about many kinds of men, returns us to the point of departure on a higher plane.

White's concept is, however, not concerned with the mechanics of evolution. These can only be laid bare by analyzing evolutionary sequences in segments of the total process, studying each such sequence in its own terms, in terms of its connection in time with other sequences following it, or in terms of its comparability with other sequences occurring at other places and times. Julian H. Steward, coming to a professorship at Columbia University from the editorship of the *Handbook of South American Indians,* stressed the need for the empirical investigation of particular evolutionary sequences. Asking for a "multilineal" approach to evolution, he emphasized those sequences of parallel development that he could establish empirically, such as the repeated development of the same forms of social and political organization among certain kinds of hunters and gatherers, the parallel development of the great societies based on irrigation, the parallel development of horse-riding nomads in North and South America as the result of the introduction of the horse to the western hemisphere, the parallel emergence of similar social and economic patterns among rubber tappers in the Amazon Basin and the fur trappers of the American North. Many of his influential writings have appeared in collected form in his *Theory of Culture Change* (1955).

Yet Steward still confined his approach to the study of particular sequences of parallel development, neglecting to apply the perspective of evolution either to the development of unique sequences or to the consideration of the general, universal evolutionary process. This additional step became possible when Marshall D. Sahlins and Elman R. Service of the University of Michigan presented additional arguments in their *Evolution and Culture* (1960), which bears a preface by White. Here they distinguished between general and specific evolution. General evolution, they argued, refers to the successive emergence of new levels of all-round development. But this emergence is produced by the historic interplay of many cultures and culture sequences. Some of these cultures and culture sequences may be unique; others may exhibit parallelisms that occur several times over. Some may make a strategic contribution to the cumulative evolutionary process; others may stagnate. Some may, like Eskimo culture, become increasingly and ever more narrowly adapted to an inhospitable environment, sacrificing their potential for future development to an efficient fit with the environment. Others, like the irrigation societies of the Near East or of Peru, may fall by the wayside, after handing on their skills, their social patterns, their ideas, to another. Sahlins and Service call the development of such connected historic forms specific evolution. Some, but not all, of these specific sequences are seen to be the incubators and carriers of the general process. But all may be seen in the perspective of evolution.

Thus Steward, Sahlins, and Service emphasized the importance of studying particular sequences of forms, a traditional concern of American anthropology. But their emphasis is no more of a return to the antievolutionist particularism of the prewar period than the study of isolated biological systems projected against a backdrop of Darwinian evolution represents a return to the study of isolated Linnean archetypes. We are in fact learning not to sacrifice the general for the particular, nor the particular to the general. Particularism often has a special appeal to Americans, raised in an empiricist intellectual tradition. Its special danger lies in the propensity to accumulate facts like so many grains of sand to produce merely bigger and bigger sand piles. Generality without particularism, on the other hand, tends to abstract from questions of mechanism, and thus to fall into the opposite danger of imputing an autonomous cumulative motion to phenomena that can propel the intellectual enterprise straight into Plato's cave. Both extremes are the products of impatience, of the wish to obtain "hard" results, coupled with an intolerance for inconsistencies and uncertainties, which are not merely unavoidable in the study of a complex subject matter but which constitute its inherent appeal.

The new American evolutionism may, therefore, represent the achievement of a degree of scientific maturity. It must face its own special problems, of course, such as its free use of biological concepts like adaptation, dominance, specialization, or fitness. Such a conceptual apparatus bears the mark of a resurrected Social Darwinism, stripped of the imperialist racism that marked it in the nineteenth century, but resurgent in the new Realpolitik of our transition to the second millenium. The employment of analogies drawn from biology is consistent with the naturalistic bias of American anthropology. The possible limitation of such analogies derives from the fact that culture is not an organism. A society is not a whole composed of specialized cells, but an organization of bodily and mentally distinct individuals who must learn to synchronize their actions with each other in a complex interplay of cooperation and conflict. A culture is not a preset genetic code, allowing for variation only through a mistake in the coding, but a body of materials—material, social, and ideal forms—to which new material may be added and from which old material may be lost. The human design allows of vastly increased autonomy of action in the individual, and vastly increased heterogeneity in the codes by which individuals learn to act together.

Yet there will be those who bridle at the terms employed in the preceding paragraph, such terms as *design* or *code*. Indeed, their usage bespeaks the major shift in anthropology during the period that I am considering in this essay. Increasingly, we find ourselves using not the language of subjective involvement with the primitive, but the language of the engineer. The image of man projected by current anthropology is indeed an engineer's image. To a consideration of this image we must now turn, for such images are not neutral. The meaning of meaning lies in its uses, and the uses by anthropologists and others of this new projection of man and his capabilities is fraught with serious consequences both for its users and those upon whom it is used.

HUMAN DESIGN AND CULTURAL CODE

The previous chapter examined—however briefly—some of the changes that distinguish postwar anthropology in America from its prewar phase. This chapter is to examine the vision of man that is projected by current American anthropology. In this concern, anthropology and the humanities impinge most directly upon each other, however much scholars may wish to shield themselves from contact through the use of esoteric vocabularies.

I have referred earlier to the shift from an interest in the gamut of human variability as expressed in the multiplicity of human cultures to the attempt to define some underlying reality beneath the ever changing surface of human phenomena, to delineate the common psychobiological structure of man, to specify the common blueprint of the human animal. In prewar anthropology, the psychobiological design of man seemed irrelevant. The design was open; it could be made to subscribe to any culture. Cultural variability, unhampered by limitations of physique or psyche, seemed endless. In the postwar period, the design appeared closed. Much as the inherited genes are thought by some to dictate our adult characteristics, so the inherited design of man forced men over and over again to seek answers to the same questions, solutions to the same innate needs. At best, these answers might be seen as varying slightly from cultural setting to cultural setting, secondary variations upon the same basic themes, sounding with monotonous regularity.

No better indicator of this change can be found than the innovative work of Margaret Mead. A student of Boas at Columbia University, she first went into the field to investigate adolescence in Samoa and returned to emphasize the cross-cultural variability of the adolescent period in her *Coming of Age in Samoa* (1928). Her emphasis on the cultural variability of human nature reached its peak in her comparison of three New Guinea tribes in *Sex and Temperament in Three Primitive Societies* (1935). Among the first of these, the Arapesh, both sexes were shown as equally nurturant; among the second, the fierce Mundugumor, both sexes were equally aggressive. Among the third, the Tchambuli, the relation between the sexes stereotyped in Western culture appeared reversed. In these portrayals, as in her portrayals of many other cultures, the uniqueness of each culture was stressed and vividly presented through great skill in research and description. Yet in *Male and Female,* written in 1947, there appeared a renewed emphasis on the irreducible differences between the sexes. And in recent years, as she has shown in her self-evaluation entitled "Retrospects and Prospects" (1962), she has returned to the consideration of a layer of human behavior so basic and universal that cultural modification is minimal. Specifically, this reappraisal has involved a return also to the consideration of Sigmund Freud's *Totem and Taboo,* his inspired fantasy on the origin of the incest taboo.

This book might almost serve as an indicator of the pendulum swing in anthropological thinking. In 1920, Alfred L. Kroeber had reacted negatively against the book in a review which—in Freud's own words—characterized it as a Just So story. Thereafter, most anthropologists found satisfaction in Malinowski's confrontation of the Oedipal theory with material drawn from his experience with the Trobriand Islanders, and his conclusion—expressed in his *Sex and Repression in Savage Society* (1927)—that the psychological complexes formed in the process of maturation were culturally relative. Freud, Malinowski argued, had based his conclusions on the study of patients drawn from a society that traced descent through fathers, and where the father combined authority over the son with the right of sexual access to the mother. Here, then, the son had to rebel against the father, both in his role as a figure of authority and as a monopolist of mother's sexual favors. In a matrilineal society like that of the Trobriand Islanders, however, descent was traced through the mother. The person exercising authority over the son was not father, but mother's brother, who—at the same time—was barred from sexual access to his sister, the boy's mother. Father, on the other hand, though a competitor for mother's favors, was an outsider where mother's descent group was concerned, and deprived of any authority over mother's people, including his own son. Therefore, where authority and sexual monopoly combined to create Oedipal difficulties in western Europe, in the Trobriands authority and sexual functions were split, lending the Oedipal involvement a quite different character. Malinowski concluded, therefore, that it was necessary "not to assume the universal existence of the Oedipus complex, but in studying every type of civilization, to establish the special complex which pertains to it."

Yet, in 1939, a return to the problem was presaged by Kroeber in his essay on Freud's "Totem and Taboo in Retrospect," later included in his *The Nature of Culture* (1952).

Kroeber proposed that, stripped of "certain gratuitous and really irrelevant assumptions," Freud's thoughts on the subject could yet prove "fertile in the realm of cultural understanding instead of being mainly rejected or coldly ignored as a brilliant fantasy." And in 1951 Clyde Kluckhohn, whose own position on the question was mixed when he began fieldwork among the Indians of the American Southwest, could write in "Some Notes on Navaho Dreams" that "facts uncovered in my own fieldwork and that of my collaborators have forced me to the conclusion that Freud and other psychoanalysts have depicted with astonishing correctness many central themes in motivational life which are universal. The styles of expression of these themes and much of the manifest content are culturally determined, but the underlying psychologic drama transcends cultural difference." (*Psychoanalysis and Culture,* 1951, ed. George B. Wilbur and Warner Muensterberger, p. 120.) Once again anthropologists found themselves fascinated by the picture of man's prolonged period of dependency—his long prenatal incubation, his postnatal helplessness, his long-delayed and difficult maturation.

Anthropologists also found themselves once again engaged in tasks long laid aside, in attempts to define recurrent reactions of the human psyche to situations of the same general order. In the 1860's Adolf Bastian, a German ethnographer, had attempted to define a body of ideas common to all men, the so-called *Elementargedanken* or basic ideas. As cultural variability was emphasized, this attempt had fallen into disuse, living on perhaps only in such latter-day formulations as Jung's universal archetypes. With the renewed stress on the psychic unity of mankind, the attempt revived, and in 1960 Clyde Kluckhohn could again argue, in a contribution to a volume on myths and mythmaking, that "the interaction of a certain kind of biological apparatus in a certain kind of physical world with some inevitables of the human condition (the helplessness of infants, two parents of different sex, etc.) brings about regularities in the formation of imaginative productions, of powerful images" (p. 49), such as parricide, matricide, the search for the father, supernatural marriages, incest, sibling rivalry, castration, the Oedipus myth, the Orpheus myth, the concept of introjected magic causing illness and death, magical curing, magical means for overcoming space, the appearance of inexhaustible food supplies, magical weapons for the conquest of rivals, animals as characters in stories, were-animals, creation myths, the myth of the hero, the myth of the eternal return, catastrophes, and androgynous deities. And the anthropologist and folklorist, Alan Dundes has proposed, in a 1962 article, "Earth-Diver: Creation of the Mythopoeic Male," that it may therefore not be sufficient to interpret myth as reflecting the functional integration of the particular culture where the myth was collected, at the time it was collected, since many myths are much older than the culture in which they were encountered and often transcend the cultural boundaries of the unit of collection.

What is true of myths has also been asserted to be true of dreams. As in the case of myths, the "underlying psychological drama" is seen as producing over and over again similar symbolic forms in the dreams of men born into quite different cultures. Examples of this are the equation of wealth with feces, of death with the loss of a tooth, of birth with water. Similarly, the supposition that men everywhere project themselves emotionally upon their environment in the same way has led to analyses of non-Western and primitive art forms

37

as projective forms, created in the same manner by beings possessed of the same psychobiological denominator. These studies are as ingenious as they are intriguing. In the first of these Anthony Wallace, in "A Possible Technique for Recognizing Psychological Characteristics of the Ancient Maya from an Analysis of Their Art" (1950), applied the scoring categories used in a variety of psychological tests, especially in the Rorschach "ink-blot" test, to the three extent pictorial manuscripts of the Maya of Yucatan. He then matched his findings against the interpretations of psychological tests applied to a Maya-speaking group in highland Guatemala, to encounter an almost perfect accord. Similarly, but independently, George T. Mills, in his *Navaho Art and Culture* (1959), first presents a formal analysis of Navaho artistic performance and products in four kinds of media: the production of paintings made on the ground with many-colored sands; weaving; silver work; and free hand drawing. He then consults the literature of Euro-American psychology for generalizations on the relation between personality types and artistic representations, and applies these hypotheses to the recurrent elements and patterns of elements, established in the course of his formal analysis, and set off against the characterizations of the Navaho made by anthropologists. Again, we encounter a surprising consistency between art forms, psychological characterization, and anthropological reporting.

Where the older anthropology, therefore, tended to see variability, postwar anthropology has tended to see a uniform plot, modified in particular instances only by a particular cultural "phrasing." The basic plot is that of a suffering humanity, forever living under the shadow of a painful and regressive infantilism. The cultural phrasings of this plot form the particular code through which a particular group of fellow-sufferers communicate both their fellow-suffering and their defenses against it. This view implies a new version of the old theory of the social contract. According to the old theory, human actors contract among themselves to maintain a social order for their mutual benefit. The current theory reproduces this contractual paradigm, but the times have changed and the original versions of the contract have suffered metamorphosis.

It is no longer a Hobbesian compact that is envisaged, according to which men lay down their arms, lest each man's hand be raised against every other. Nor is it a Lockean compact to guarantee the integrity of each man's property and maximal liberty. Today, rather, the contract is seen as an agreement to communicate, each man not a keeper of his fellow's safety or property, but of his social and emotional integrity. Thus, for example, Erving Goffman has, in his "The Nature of Deference and Demeanor" (1956), painted a brilliant picture of how the self is delineated continuously anew, as it presents an appropriate image of itself to others, who, by paying the image deference, complete it. He sees the self as a ceremonial thing, a sacred object that must be treated with proper ritual care and that in turn must be presented in proper light to others. Hence no man is an island, and society is forever engaged in the ceremonial labor of undoing and shoring up these individual fragile selves. For the self is seen as a fragile reed, easily broken when the appropriate ceremonial communication is brought to a standstill.

While Clyde Kluckhohn and the more psychoanalytically oriented anthropologists have stressed the common emotional drama of man, another group of anthropologists has laid emphasis on the commonality of human cognitive capacities. To support culture at all, Anthony Wallace has argued in his "The Psychic Unity of Human Groups" (1961), men must be able to perform several psychological functions, such as perception, memory, discrimination between perceived and remembered stimuli, continuous scanning of all such stimuli, discrimination between sets of stimuli with respect to their meaning, and a capacity to match these meanings with overt responses. To accomplish this, man must maintain a minimal semantic capacity, a capacity for minimal distinctions; and Wallace suggests that there may be a low level of this capacity below which men could not maintain the complex tasks required of them in known human cultures. He points to the interesting finding that folk taxonomies, such as kinship terminologies or military rankings, tend to make their distinctions in terms of about four or five binary discriminations, and he feels that the ability to make this modicum of distinctions may very well be close to the minimum level of cognitive capacity required of man as an animal with culture. While Wallace himself disagrees sharply with those who would seek a common human denominator in the commonality of emotions, he too emphasizes a common property of humankind. His model of man is not that of the human sufferer, forever experiencing the regressive pull of early experiences, but the robot, possessed of a brain of sufficient capacity to function as a simple computer, responding to the particular discriminations of the cultural code to which it has been cued. His vision of the social compact is not that of a society of potentially regressive selves, engaged in the ceremonial labor of communicating through a common code of cultural phrasings, but human machines, connected in a network, equipped to make the same cognitive discriminations in the same order. Despite these differences in orientation and feeling tone, both approaches treat culture as a code for communication between individuals who must synchronize their separate and disparate lives.

In this phrasing of culture as a code, one may discern the twin influences of communication engineering and modern linguistics. Certainly we cannot escape the impact of mass communication, nor the effects of the explosive growth of information storage devices and communication systems. The appeal of linguistics to many anthropologists, on the other hand, lies in its ability to formulate the basic elements and organizing principles of a given language in elegantly simple ways. It has thus become easy for us to think of the social process as involving continuous communication between actors, and to conceive of culture on the analogy of a linguistic code through which communication is effected. To realize the novelty of this point of view it is only necessary to leaf through the older definitions of culture, most of which follow Edward Tylor's (1871) view of culture as an aggregate, "as that complex whole which includes knowledge, belief, art, law, morals, custom, and any other capabilities and habits acquired by man as a member of society." Such definitions stress things, ideas, social arrangements in all their materiality. The newer definitions are, by comparison, literally ethereal.

One of the major current American attempts to utilize a linguistic model for cultural analysis is the anthropological study of values. Despite the fact that the technical study of non-Western languages has tended to occupy a peripheral rather than a central place in the repertoire of anthropological disciplines, linguistic models have always had considerable influence over the theoretical formulations in cultural anthropology (see David F. Aberle's article on "The Influence of Linguistics on Early Culture and Personality Theory," 1960). Linguists like Edward Sapir (1884-1939)—engaged in building linguistic codes from minimal sets of basic building blocks, phonemes—probably influenced, or at least paralleled, the Benedictian view of culture as selecting a limited number of features from the vast arc of human possibilities. Benedict's "pattern" concept still focused on recurrence and regularities of behavior in different contexts of the same culture; Kluckhohn's notion of culture as a "design" for living, however, invites an attempt to specify the "design features" of a culture. With this idea we enter the realm of communication engineering and codification.

Kluckhohn's explicit application of linguistic thinking to cultural codification took its departure from an initial question, raised explicitly in 1956 in an article on "Toward a Comparison of Value-Emphases in Different Cultures." "How," he asked, "can we compare with minimal ethnocentrism the more general or thematic value-tones or value-emphases that constitute the structure-points of whole systems of cultural values?" The model selected to answer this question is linguistic. "Just as all phonemic systems include nasals, stops, and sibilants of a limited variety of types, so all value systems place their weightings on the desirable relations to nature, other individuals, and self within a describable set of alternatives." The total range of alternatives is limited; but each value code represents a selection from the total arc of alternative possibilities. In values, "as in grammar or in a phonological system, there are a comparatively small number of basic principles, the influence of which may be detected in wide ranges of content." The aim thus becomes the formulation of a set of grammars of human cultures. Just as the function of linguistic grammar "is to control the freedom of words so that there is no needless congestion of communication traffic," so "the 'grammar' of each culture likewise provides the necessary minimum of orderliness." The value code, moreover, is here seen as the superorganic equivalent of the genetic code in the organic realm. Where lower organisms are constrained from within by mechanisms that are built in genetically, a creature such as man—capable of displacement to an inordinate degree—must be constrained from without, through a "grammar" of conduct.

The approach has strong appeal to anthropologists, not only because it is consistent with many assumptions we make regarding the nature of man and culture, but also because, as Alfred Kroeber says in *The Nature of Culture* (1952), it allows us to study "values as natural phenomena occurring in nature—much like the characteristic forms, qualities, and abilities of animals as defined in comparative zoology." "Such study has actually been made, time and again, often without explicit awareness of values being involved, and perhaps as often without awareness that the study has natural scientific significance."

But the value approach has one major deficiency, its tendency to divorce valuation from the context of valuation, to render reality irrelevant to the process by which men employ values. To describe etiquette or values as a code means to deal with the signals men use in relating themselves to each other, not with the relationships themselves. A code is a language of signs; how that language is utilized is a different matter. The point is relevant not merely to the study of culture. In his recent paper on "The Ethnography of Speaking" (1962), Dell H. Hymes has made the same point with regard to the study of language. The analysis of the structure of a linguistic code is not identical with the functions of speech. He too has pointed to the fact that when a linguistic code is treated in the abstract, a given linguistic form is seen as associated with a range of meanings, representing an optimum of possibility. But "when a form is used in a context, it eliminates the meanings possible to that context other than those that form can signal; the context eliminates from consideration the meanings possible to the form other than those that context can support." Hence we must draw a distinction between formal meaning and effective meaning, just as we must draw a distinction between formal values and effective values. To know what effective meanings are present "the analysis must be made on the ground. We must know what patterns are available in what contexts, and how, where and when they come into play. The maxim that 'meaning is use' has new force when we seriously study the role of semantic habits in behavior" (p. 20).

If meaning is use, then we must know not only what the grammar of appropriate behavior in a culture may be; we must also attempt to discover what relationships—economic, political, legal, ritual—are sheathed in the symbolic covering of the code. These relationships are, however, rarely uniform and unitary. Instead men respond to the challenges of real life by throwing up various patterns and social arrangements, by developing different strategies and different "programs." In doing so, they may make use of the same code, but—as the British social anthropologist Edmund Leach has pointed out in his brilliant study of *Political Systems in Highland Burma*

44

(1954)—different versions of the same code, different stances in the performance of the same ritual may signify great disparities in the conflicting claims over resources and power. Codes are used to activate quite different mechanisms in the social structure, to play quite different social games. The social engineer who sees all members of a society as "coded" to the same inputs reduces them to the status of faceless puppets whose passivity underwrites the continuation of the system. He does not see the labor of men engaged in life.

Another group of anthropologists, similarly abstracting code from context, have erred in the opposite direction. They have seen men not as totally faceless, but as totally free. Studies of valuation, divorced from the contexts in which such valuations occur, may conjure up visions of human culture in the shape of a bazaar, offering a plethora of opportunities. Individuals or whole cultures are then represented as "selecting" values from a range of values, much as the individual shopper selects nylons or cookies in a supermarket. This is the way, for instance, that Otto von Mering has approached the problem in his *A Grammar of Human Values* (1961). Making a study of how individuals make judgments of value among the Navaho of Rimrock and the Texan American settlers of Homestead, he has drawn his basic assumptions about the valuation process from the existentialist philosophy of Kierkegaard. He posits that "at the inception of the valuation process—at the time when the individual contemplates and begins to select values appropriate to some intended conduct—a potential cultural reservoir of *many* possible values is theoretically within the reach of every person. Thus, initially for the individual the optimum relationship attainable to values is one of possibility." Similarly, Florence R. Kluckhohn and Fred L.

45

Strodtbeck, in their *Variations in Value Orientations* (1961), have posited all values to be potentially present in a culture at the same time, yet with some values exercising dominance over others. They thus visualize an optimum relationship of possibility to values for whole cultures, in the way Mering posited it for individuals. But—and this is a criticism directed at all existentialist views that separate the evaluating individual from the context in which the valuations take place—the relation of evaluator to values is never an optimum relation of possibility, but a minimum relation of necessity. In any given society men value what they must value, and alternatives in valuation do not stem from the individual wishes so much as from the exigencies of the situation. Values relate not to some hypothetical optimum offering of cultural wares, but to the limited necessary tasks a culture must fulfill under a given set of circumstances. The problem of understanding culture is not exhausted by the concept of coding, because men are not "caught upon the hook of socialization" or "broken upon the wheel of culture"; they are capable of using the materials of culture to respond in alternative ways to the challenges of a given situation. Yet—and this is equally important—these alternative responses are not limitless. They represent alternative strategies in the face of necessity.

What is true of groups in society is true also of the individual in a social setting. There is a dynamic interplay between the individual and the materials of his life, just as there is a dynamic interplay between social groups and the circumstances of their existence. There is an all too facile determinism in the view that sees men as mere repetitive copies of the same human design, or in the complementary notion that men are coded like IBM cards in the course of socialization.

Men are not merely the victims of a repetitive psychological drama, nor coded dummies. They are capable also of using the materials provided by their culture to *grow on*. Men use the things, the patterns of behavior, the images of their culture, to make and remake themselves continuously. Let us not forget that to this day neither psychology nor psychoanalysis possesses a satisfactory theory of maturation, only a sophisticated understanding of man's multiple immaturities. But we must think of what men are and can be not merely in the image of illness, but also in the image of health.

If men are capable of projecting endlessly the wounds inflicted on them in the course of maturation, they are capable also of using their projections as guideposts and blueprints of their own identity. Freud not only pointed out that men project in order to protect themselves, by converting internal stimuli into seemingly outer events. He also saw that men are, in his phrasing, incapable of imposing the artifice of formal art on their internal sensations from within alone. They accomplish this by rendering their internal world external. Once externalized, it is public—it can be shared among men, and communicated between men. Thus myths, as Jerome Bruner has pointed out in an essay on "Myth and Identity" (1960), are not only projections of human wishes and fantasies; myth may also be the tutor, the shaper of identities. "One may speak," he says, "of the corpus of myth as providing a possible set of programmatic identities for the individual personality. It would perhaps be more appropriate to say that the mythologically instructed community provides its members with a library of scripts upon which the individual may judge the internal drama of his multiple identities." Dorothy Eggan, long a pioneer in the collection and analysis of dreams among primitives in general and the Hopi in particular, has made the same point in her recent summary statement on "Dream Analysis" (1961): "The dream process, influenced by cultural beliefs, frequently gives a clear picture of a culturally constituted self-image 'walking a tight-rope' toward the mental equilibrium of ego-identity balanced by a 'pole' of culturally shared dream experience."

The same process—the periodic reshaping of man's internal identity through its periodic testing against the external cultural code—clearly underlies creativity in the arts. It is perhaps due to the easy determinism alluded to above that American anthropologists have tended to neglect the individual artist and his relation to his audience, in favor of the study of technique and art object. The last major contribution in this field was Ruth Bunzel's *The Pueblo Potter* (1929), an endeavor stimulated by Boas. Others—notably the Dutch (see, for example, A. A. Gerbrands' *Art as an Element of Culture, Especially in Negro Africa,* 1957)—have gone much further in the study of the individual native craftsman and artist at work, while Americans deserted the problem of creativity for the more mechanical study of the products of creativity.

Yet the exploration of human creativity, however humble, may well be required of us, if only to counterbalance our usual emphasis on man's determination by culture. Not only do men work incessantly at the integration of public code and private protocol; there is also evidence that they find the interplay between outward discipline and inner drive rewarding. Otherwise, how account for such human endeavors as games in which the imposition of *ad hoc* codes on play impulses is felt as pleasurable, or for man's recurrent choice of rituals to "act out" his private drives in publicly coded form, or for art? George Devereux has recently emphasized the dialectic of code and drive for us in an article on "Art and Mythology: A General Theory" in Bert Kaplan's *Studying Personality Cross-Culturally* (1961). Devereux defines art as "the straining of pure affect against pure (culturally structured) discipline, and the incidental evolving of new rules which permit the less and less roundabout manifestation of more and more affect and also of hitherto artistically unusable affect segments within an expanded, but internally even more coherent, discipline. The discipline itself—the rules of the game—is the means whereby society determines whether a given expressive act represents art or something else, and also whether the product in question is good, mediocre or bad art" (p. 362).

These remarks of Devereux caution us not to take too static a view of the human design. They warn us against seeing only the limitations and not the possibilities. This is true not only ontogenetically, where the development of the individual is concerned, but philogenetically, where we deal with the development of the entire human species. Nor are these doubts confined to the investigator who wishes to deal adequately with the fact of individual creativity. They emerge also from more general considerations, from investigations into the origin of the human design in the past, and questions that we must ask about its future. Thus, paradoxically perhaps, the question of what man *is* turns into its very opposite, the queries of how this design came to be and of what it is capable, what it may yet become.

The first of these queries, how the human design came to be, is a question about human origins and the origins of culture. Long regarded as scientifically useless, for lack of evidence that could be adduced to answer it, the question has again become scientifically respectable, with the advent of a "new" human biology. (See, for example, the symposia volumes *The Evolution of Man's Capacity for Culture,* 1959, edited by James N. Spuhler of the University of Michigan, and *Social Life of Early Man,* edited by Sherwood L. Washburn of the University of California, Berkeley.)

This new human biology treats man and his capabilities and liabilities not as a pattern *sui generis,* but as one of many patterns thrown up in the course of evolution. With a much richer body of fossil evidence than ever before, it has become possible to visualize man's biological emergence more clearly than in the past. We are also able to project man more fully against a more differentiated ecological background, filled in by vast advances in geology, climatology, and paleontology. Most important, we now know that tool using preceded the development of fully fledged modern brains, and we can infer that tool using was one of the conditions of cerebral development, not one of its effects. Thus we can now see that culture, far from coming into being only after man's biological development was complete, is actually a condition, a continuous accompaniment of human evolution. This allows us to see the human design and the tasks to which it is put in reciprocal relationship, one pacing the other, rather than an immutable quantity upon which new unprecedented tasks are imposed. We need look no longer for a missing link who stepped out upon the stage of history with all human capabilities full blown, like Pallas Athene from the head of Zeus. The timeless human design dissolves; there emerges instead the picture of complex ordering and rearrangement over time, producing, in the fullness of time, the temporary evolutionary arrangement that we call man.

Problems long abandoned are revived with new approaches and new techniques. Systematic comparisons of communication systems among animals and insects alike yields new knowledge of those features that specifically distinguish human communication from all other, and permit more refined questions regarding the origin of the particular capabilities that underlie human speech. Field studies of living primates in their natural habitats are beginning to teach us something of the generic social pattern that must have been instrumental in bringing about the kind of associations characteristic of human beings. At the same time, there is a burgeoning of new approaches to the study of the incest taboo—that specifically human cultural complex that forces humans to seek mates outside the group into which they were born, and thus extends, by fiat, the bonds of human association beyond the isolated band of immediate kin. While none of these approaches has been wholly successful, all of them are suggestive, whether they base their explanations on ecological considerations, on the lengthening of the primate life cycle in the course of human evolution, on the relations of inbreeding to fertility, on the role of the mother in socially isolated families, on communication theory, or on the role of the family within the larger society. Some fifteen years ago A. Irving Hallowell, of the University of Pennsylvania—in "Personality Structure and the Evolution of Man," his presidential address before the American Anthropological Association in 1949—drew attention to the special psychological capabilities of man, his possession of a conscious and evaluating self, which underlie and accompany the elaboration of culture.

From the studies stimulated by the renewed emphasis in anthropology on the human design as closed and limited there has emerged a sense of the human animal as ever changing in response to the conditions of his life, and in interaction with them. Similarly, culture has come to be regarded as an emergent, prompted into existence by the reciprocal relation of this animal with his world. The relationship of man to this world is neither one of abject servitude nor one of unlimited possibility, but one of continuous confrontation of limitations, and a slow transcendence thereof. This is a perspective that the engineering approach to culture and to the individual in culture causes us to forget. If it is true, as Lévi-Strauss once said in conversation, that "anthropology begins with people and ends with people, but in between there is plenty of room for computers," let us take heed not to reverse this dictum, to see men as the intervening links between machines. Let us remember that if men live under conditions of limited possibilities these possibilities are the stuff of which they *make* their lives. It is the obligation of anthropologists to describe and analyze these active interchanges with the real world, while retaining a sense of human partnership for the men we study. In this obligation, anthropology as a science and anthropology as a humanity are one.

◄§ 3 §►

THE TRANSFORMATION OF CULTURE

If the human design cannot take shape except through the mediation of culture, then the discussion is returned to the concept of culture, the concept *sine qua non* of the anthropologist. But, I shall suggest, we are confronting a concept vastly different in shape and meaning from the concept that occupied the anthropologist at an earlier time. This is perhaps least apparent at the level of practical inquiry where the field anthropologist carries on his traditional transactions with the reality he wishes to understand, whether this be the reality of Haitian market women higgling over the price of onions, Hanunoo in the Philippines joshing each other in joking songs, or members of the Subanum tribe involved in the diagnosis of illness. Yet even such particular endeavors of the anthropologist are subject to the new perspectives in which the particulars are visualized, and hence will suffer a transformation as cases are studied from new points of view.

The fact is that the concept of culture no longer denotes a watertight category, clearly separate and separable from similarly watertight categories, such as The Environment or Man as an Organism. We have moved on to emphasize interrelationships, and to visualize chains of systems within systems, rather than isolated phenomena with impermeable boundaries. Even when particular investigators single out one aspect of reality for intensive consideration, they are aware—much more aware than in the past—that abstraction, the "taking out" of context, involves a complementary action, in which the abstracted phenomenon is returned to its "ground." We are less willing to assert that culture possesses this or that absolute attribute, that it *is* a mechanical sum of culture traits, or that it *is* like an organism, more willing to consider that it may be *thought of* as a sum of culture traits, or as an organism, depending on the appropriate context. The statements made about culture or cultures now include the observer, and the observer has grown sophisticated in his knowledge that there may be other positions of vantage from which the object may be viewed, and that he may himself occupy successive points of vantage in approaching his "object" of study. Any object can thus be seen as belonging to multiple systems: a human population may be considered as carriers of a culture, related to other cultures in both space and time; or as breeding ground for microorganisms that prey on it; or as agents of ecological disequilibrium when its members fire the forest cover in pursuit of game or prepare the soil for cultivation. Each aspect, singled out for analysis, may be viewed in its particular systematic characteristics, its orderliness in which a change in one part reacts on other parts; but the systems intertwine so that one system represents a component in another that, in turn, may form the coordinate of still a third.

With this shift of emphasis, traditional antinomies are giving way to relational categories. We may, for example, still speak heuristically of biology *and* culture, but the two categories merge in such studies as that by Frank B. Livingstone of the University of Michigan on "Anthropological Implications of Sickle Cell Gene Distribution in West Africa" (1958). Livingstone shows how the Negro farmers who invaded the tropical forest of West Africa cleared and burned the tree cover to obtain land for cultivation, while at the same time establishing permanent habitation sites. This in turn spurred the rise of holoendemic malaria, which set up selective pressures favoring a wider distribution of the sickle cell gene, which—if inherited from one parent but not both—offers immunity to malaria. Possession of the sickle cell gene then, in turn, permitted populations having it to enter malarial country. Similarly, we no longer speak of culture and environment as if these were two separate hostile categories. This opposition of terms has given way to the study of cultural ecology, pioneered by Julian H. Steward, who devised a strategy for discovering what relationships exist and what consequences these relationships entail for the remainder of culture. This strategy is a method, not a theory. It differs from either environmental determinism, which strives to explain culture in terms of its environment, or cultural determinism, which explains the adaptation to the environment purely as a result of culture, by making the question of how a particular technology is used in a particular environment an open one. Social organization appears no longer as a category *sui generis,* opposed to categories like material culture or ideology, but as a complex process by which groups of people within societies and between societies relate themselves to each other or differentiate themselves from each other in the setting of available resources. We no longer set off one culture against another, but include them both in "social fields" or "interaction areas," or—with Alfred L. Kroeber—in the spatially and historically interconnected growth of civilization, or—with Leslie White—as a temporary segment of a global stream of interacting and interconnected cultural elements and constellations of culture elements.

55

All of these ways of looking at culture point away from an absorption in particular cultural facts, restricted in space and time, toward an emerging view of the cultural process as ultimately universal. Alfred L. Kroeber attempted his most explicit formulation of this unity in his concept of the Oikumene, presented in the Huxley Memorial Lecture for 1945 and included in his essays, *The Nature of Culture* (1952, pp. 379-95). There he said:

> The Greeks gave the name Oikumene, "the inhabited," to their supposed total habitable world stretching from the Pillars of Hercules to the Indians and the Seres. Since centuries, of course, this term has proved no longer to correspond to its original extent of meaning. But the tract referred to by the Greeks does still correspond to a great historic unit, to a frame within which a particular combination of processes happened to achieve certain unique results. Especially, the forces at work there managed to achieve the most important forms of civilization as yet produced by mankind. The old name Oikumene, with a partial shift of meaning from the "range of mankind" to "range of man's most developed cultures," thus remains a convenient designation for an interwoven set of happenings and products which are significant equally for the culture historian and for the theoretical anthropologist.

In traditional manner Kroeber traced the geographical distribution of culture complexes—such as agriculture, domesticated animals, the divinity of kingship, eunuchism, divinatory practices, alchemy, the great religions, cavalry, felt, chess, and printing—across the body of the Old World. The facts of their distribution, he felt, enabled him to see the Oikumene of the Old World as "a great web of culture growth, really extensive and rich in content," woven together by the spread of material and ideology. Moreover, no longer were the primitives, surviving in the interstices or along the margins of this great arena of culture building, seen in glorious isolation. They, too, he held, "derive their cultures mainly from the civilization characteristic of the Oikumene as a whole, through reductive selection. They preserve old elements largely discarded elsewhere, and they do without elements which their retardation makes them unable or unwilling to accept."

It was perhaps characteristic of Kroeber that he would deal primarily and most easily with bits of culture, paying little or no attention to the types of social orders and their intercommunications that structured the transmission of cultural bits from one area of the Oikumene to another. Yet his vision of the essential historical unity of Old World culture, a unity created by the dynamic interplay of the very particularisms that composed it, sounded a theme of moment. It was not long before the archaeologist Gordon R. Willey, whose work had led him from the interpretation of the cultural development of the eastern United States to considerations of the culture sequences in Peru and in Middle America and their possible relationships, applied the concept of an oikumene— a geographically and historically interconnected zone of cultural events—also to the western hemisphere, in a paper on "The Prehistoric Civilizations of Nuclear America" (1955). Viewed historically, the Spanish foray into the American Caribbean thus marked the closure of a world system of culture, of which the interconnected units could be seen as the component parts.

In similar terms—especially in "The Individual and the Culture Process"—Leslie White had long been speaking of a universal culture process as

57

a stream of interconnected cultural elements—of instruments, beliefs, customs, etc. In this interactive process, each element impinges upon others and is in turn acted upon by them. The process is a competitive one: instruments, customs, and beliefs may become obsolete and eliminated from the stream. New elements are incorporated from time to time. New combinations and syntheses—inventions and discoveries—of cultural elements are continually being formed . . . (p. 76).

The formulation resembles Kroeber's, though White, the evolutionist, stressed the competitiveness of cultural elements in a process of cultural selection, which produced a discernible movement toward the ever greater and more efficient harnessing of energy, while Kroeber, the historian, stressed the emergence, now here, now there, of the great aggregates of forms he called civilizations. White spoke of the general process by which man moved from savagery to civilization. Kroeber stressed the repeated local emergence, within the bubbling cultural mass, of sets of elements, characterized—as he saw them—by striking tendencies toward selectivity, toward internal consistency, toward style (see his posthumous *Roster of Civilization and Culture,* 1962). While the two men differed in their approaches to the study of the cultural process, both taught their adherents to think in large, imaginative, integrative terms.

This generalizing emphasis was also that of Robert Redfield, of the University of Chicago, whose general sociological orientation and specific fieldwork in Middle America had similarly taught him to think of the development of mankind in global terms, as a movement from the close-knit, homogeneous life of the primitive band or village to the open, heterogeneous life of the city. Where White had stressed the directionality of the process toward the maximization of energy-capture, where Kroeber had spoken of the almost sportive groping for style that characterized now this, now that assemblage of elements within the cultural stream, Redfield emphasized the qualitative change involved in the passage from primitive society to civilization. He saw the primitive and peasant society, the society of the folk, as small, isolated, homogeneous, self-sufficient; formed in the image of kinship relations, based on the face-to-face interaction of men; its culture as a body of warmly shared common understandings; the understandings thought to be permanent and sacred. Civilization, on the other hand, he wrote in *The Primitive World and Its Transformation* (1953), was not only things added to society, such as cities, writing, public works, the state, the market. It meant also a vast increase in heterogeneity, exemplified by a greatly diversified division of labor; the replacement of personal ties by impersonal relationships; the supplanting of familial connections by political affiliation or contract; the spread of reflective and systematic thought.

Thus Kroeber, White, and Redfield, each in his own way, returned American anthropology to an ancestral problem, each breaking away from the relativistic anthropology of the past, for which each and every culture represented a qualitatively unique and irreducible monad. In their varying ways, they have returned anthropology to the central concern of Lewis Henry Morgan and the evolutionists, to a view of the cultural process as universal, moving along a continuum from *societas* to *civitas,* from primitive to civil society.

Yet in their formulations all three men avoided, again each in his own way, the question of *how* the transition from primitive culture to civilization had taken place, the question of mechanism. Kroeber's natural-historical penchant is well-known. No better example of it exists than the essay on "Salt, Dogs, Tobacco" that he included in his *Nature of Culture* (pp. 263-82) to demonstrate how distributional data on the use of salt, dogs, and tobacco in native North America could be used to reconstruct local history, to assess the varying responses of two hundred-odd small societies to the spread of the same elements. Similarly, in *The Structure of Twana Culture with Comparative Notes on the Structure of Yurok Culture* (1960), which he wrote with W. W. Elmendorf, he went painstakingly through a point-by-point comparison of the culture traits common to the two cultures, to allow the scant differentiating traits to stand out in sharper relief. His ultimate ordering of cultural forms, however, was always in terms of style, not in terms of cultural components, organized to solve the on-going life problems of people. He made some important and lasting contributions to the study of social structure (e.g., *The Nature of Culture,* pp. 175-86), but, combining a strong sense for things with a sense of artistic unity in their arrangement, he had less sympathy for the delineation of the social arrangements through which men deal with men in relation to things.

Redfield, similarly, appreciated the importance of social structure and ecology (see, e.g., *The Little Community,* 1955), but his view of social structure was devoid of a sense of the dynamic interrelationships of social groups, and his view of ecology more concerned with how men view nature than with how they master nature or are mastered by it in turn. His definition of culture as "shared understandings" bespoke his profound interest in world view and its consistencies and inconsistencies; and he made an enduring contribution to the study of communication in culture. But it was the ideological process in culture that drew his attention rather than the material process of men coping with their world, by means of their culture. The understanding of the process of cultural development, however, must involve not only a knowledge of aggregated forms, of style, or of world view, but also a sense of the relation between environment and culture, of the struggle of social groups and their dynamic accommodation to one another, and, implicitly, of the emergence, distribution, and containment of power in a system. The differentiation of civilizations from the surrounding primitive world involved all of these facets, and signaled their radical transformation. We are still confronted with the task of discovering how this differentiation and transformation came about.

Leslie White's disregard of how, in fact, the evolutionary direction was imparted to the jostling stream of culture elements produced a similar gap between the view of the general process and the understanding of its particular mechanism. For White, no systematic connection existed between the general process of culture and the particular assemblages of cultural elements that made up particular cultures, localized in a time and place. This gap is most evident in White's own writings, which consist, on the one hand, of courageous attempts to define and clarify the nature of the cultural process and, on the other hand, of careful ethnographies of individual cultural assemblages among the Indians of the Southwest, very much in the Boasian tradition. Predictability, orderliness, law existed only within the world stream of culture, Culture with a capital *C*. A particular segment of the process, *a* culture, was to him only a temporary spatial or historical aggregate of traits.

Yet it is ultimately the interplay of cultures, in the plural, that results in the movement or stagnation of the evolutionary process, and this interplay is, in turn, dependent upon the comparative capacity of these cultures, their viability in relation to each other. Such capacity, such viability, however, is not merely a product of the sum of culture elements present in a culture, nor of its stylistic unity or intellectual integration. It is a product also of its constitution—its social organization, its harnessing of power, its internal arrangements of things, people, and ideas.

But it is precisely this aspect that has been most neglected in the work of these three anthropologists. In this they but exhibit a more general and characteristic failing of American anthropology in the prewar past. The American anthropologist seems to have felt at home either in studies of material culture, or cultural equipment, or in studies of the more elusive elements of ideology, in the search for patterns, themes, values, styles, national characteristics. But, characteristically, he has been uneasy or imprecise in his understandings of social organization, and especially in his understandings of the power aspect of social organization. These are, in turn, the fields cultivated by our British colleagues, who—on their part—have neglected studies of material culture and have felt considerable discomfort with American efforts to study "value-culture."

I have already mentioned the divergent origins of the American key concept of culture and the British key concept of society, and commented on some of the implications of this divergence. Clearly, the original intent in inquiry was different, leading scholars on the two sides of the Atlantic in different directions. Nor is it too much to say that Americans have had some difficulty in thinking about phenomena like class and power, as long as the experience of class differences and power differential had to be denied in favor of an ideology holding that everybody is middle class and that power is potentially accessible to all. The over-all result of this divergence has been a strange division of labor in the advancement of knowledge, in which the Americans have covered the low ground of culture and its high ground, whereas the British have covered the intervening middle ground. As a consequence, much American work has showed a combination of admirable precision in dealing with "things on the ground" with considerable vagueness in general interpretation, while the British have exhibited a powerful capacity to elicit details and understandings of social and political organization, which yet struck Americans as formalistic and unrelated either to "things on the ground" or to the factors which "really" make the Navaho Navaho, the Zuñi Zuñi.

This division and divergence of labor is now coming to an end—in part, because of the growing interchange of personnel and ideas between America and Britain. Both sides now have greater opportunities to view the terrain from each other's point of vantage. But Americans, at any rate, have also become more willing to consider the strategy and findings of their British colleagues, perhaps because—here, too—the experience of the war and the postwar period have reshaped our cognitions and expectations. The growing formalization of American life, sometimes of Byzantine proportions, has made us both less snide regarding British concerns and more heedful of them. And we have grown more respectful of the realities of social organization and power, even when we regard them, possibly, as more flexible and less enduring than is sometimes the case in the work of those Britishers who have emphasized equilibrium and homeostasis.

It is therefore in the middle ground of theory and investigation that we need most innovative thought. We must think of cultures in more systematic terms, and we must think of them more dynamically. We must supplement the American tendency to concentrate strongly on the formal aspects of phenomena—whether these be forms of pot rims, or forms of marriage, or concepts for dealing with the supernatural—and emphasize, with our British colleagues, what these forms do, what functions they serve in our lives. At the same time, we must not fall into the British fallacy of seeing culture and social arrangements too statically. The analogy of culture or society to an organism that has seemed congenial to them will no longer do for us, we know that cultures can borrow appropriate patterns from one another, or develop "new" organs from within, reshaping themselves to accommodate their workings to the innovation, the way a biological organism cannot. A culture may borrow or sprout wings, but a horse can do so only in fantasy. We shall instead do well not to forget Kroeber's and White's view of the culture process as a stream of components, and to think of a particular culture as a set of components that can be hooked together in different ways, to which other components may be added, or from which components may be withdrawn. Any given cultural set has a past and a future; it is the result of many experiments in arranging cultural components into workable designs.

Perhaps it is in this connection that the repression of the romantic motive, of which I have spoken in a previous chapter, will prove most beneficial. For as we suppress such longings as we may have for perfect designs, we are enabled to see that such designs as exist are temporary and provisional. "Structures," said E. Z. Vogt recently in a paper "On the Concepts of Structure and Process in Cultural Anthropology" (1960), "could then be viewed as intersections in particular time and space of a describable set of processes which involve constant change rather than movements away from or toward some kind of equilibrium" (p. 21).

Viewing structures as "intersections in particular time and space of a describable set of processes," we give primacy to the forces generating the processes; the structure becomes a temporary accommodation to these forces, which exert their pressures from within or from without the system. It is thus not enough to describe the cultural forms marking that temporary "intersection." We need to identify also the pressures and forces at work. But analysis of the cultural form itself can become meaningful only when we then view it in its *capacity* to accommodate those forces, its range of capabilities. Such a range possesses both a lower and an upper limit. The upper or lower limit may be established quantitatively, in terms of energy converted, numbers of people coordinated, or in terms of cognition yield. Qualitative analysis will tell us whether the energy or cognition yield of a given component is low or high, and whether it could be lower or higher; whether it possesses inherent limits, or whether its operation produces side effects that inhibit its intended impact.

Thus we can measure the relative capacity of a hoe made of the shoulder bone of a bison and a steel plow in the breaking of tough prairie soil. We can gage the relative carrying capacity of a territory as exploited by slash-and-burn cultivation or irrigated agriculture. We can look at kinship systems and take note of the fact that the Kariera system of Australia requires for its operation two intermarrying groups, the Arunta system four, the system of the Ambryms six. We may note that the mutual aid and security set involved in the Latin American *compadrazgo* relation, based on ceremonial sponsorship in life crisis ceremonials, is limited in scope by the number of children available for sponsorship, while a savings and loan association in a midwestern town can accommodate thousands of members. We are enabled to see how a Kachin chief attracts followers through the operations of the marriage system and the give-away, but how he cannot increase the exploitation of his sons-in-law without setting off a movement in the direction of egalitarian revolt, or how the Melanesian big-man is forced to pile feast on feast to achieve and maintain prestige, but is prevented from maximizing his role by the danger of incurring the wrath of his overtaxed followers. We grow aware of how an ancestor cult builds the solidarity of men descended from a common ancestor, but simultaneously how such adherence splits society into a series of narrow-range descent groups, each set off by its own ancestors, while a universalistic religion like Islam or Christianity possesses a wide range applicable to anyone wishing to enter the fold.

The concept of capacity thus implies performance, but also limits and contradictions, a balance of gains and costs, to be used in a new kind of social cost accounting, perhaps both more important and more promising than the economic cost accounting with which we are already familiar from our own cultural experience. Yet implicit in this view of cultural forms is also the notion that a culture will either create or borrow new and more adequate components, or be swamped by the pressures it can no longer contain.

If long-range theories make use of such concepts as oikumene or the universal cultural process, middle-range cultural theory must make use of more restricted conceptions. I have already mentioned the new concern with "social fields" and "interaction areas," in which societies are seen as interpenetrating one another, in competition and cooperation. Although these concepts are informed by a much greater sophistication about social organization and power than in the past, they do derive from concerns that were present in prewar American anthropology, even at its most particularistic. Even when culture traits appeared to travel and to assort themselves most randomly there were anthropologists like Clark Wissler (1870-1947) of the American Museum of Natural History in New York who had a strong sense of the interrelationships between culture and environment. Similarly, we must not forget that Kroeber, in the immediate prewar period, produced in his *Cultural and Natural Areas of Native North America* (published in 1939), a minute examination of the degree of overlap between cultures and environments and of their mutual relevance.

This interest has now been deepened and extended, as American anthropology in general has become more sophisticated about the mechanisms of social organization and power, and we are moving—I believe—toward a new kind of thinking in anthropology that is capable of viewing the multiple interrelationships of cultures, in balance and in conflict, in active interchanges with their environments, in much more dynamic terms than ever before. Thus the postwar period has seen the spread of cultural ecology, which—taking its departure from the work by Julian H. Steward—has asked "whether the adjustments of human societies to their environments require particular modes of behavior or whether they permit latitude for a certain range of possible behavior patterns" (*Theory of Culture Change,* p. 36). The question, first posed in Steward's own study of the Shoshonean-speaking Indians of western Colorado, Utah, Nevada, and eastern Oregon and California, his *Basin-Plateau Sociopolitical Groups* (1938), is exemplified further by Marshall D. Sahlins' *Social Stratification in Polynesia* (1958). This, says the author,

> is a study of adaptive variation in culture. It attempts to relate differences in an aspect of the social systems of aboriginal Polynesia—stratification—to differences in the adaptation of the cultures to their environments. Technology is the subsystem of culture which articulates with environment; hence, the methodology of this study consists of relating variations in social stratification to variations in technological and environmental conditions. Stratification is viewed as an aspect of social structure functionally adjusted to the technological exploitation of the environment.

Similarly, a new American social anthropology—fusing Radcliffe-Brown's functionalism with the American penchant for history—began to view social structures against the coordinates of space and time, as did Fred Eggan of the University of Chicago in his *Social Organization of the Western Pueblos* (1950).

A new archaeology, freeing itself from both the collector's madness of obtaining show pieces and from the infantile wish to restore the lost splendor of ruins long covered by earth or jungle, turned to the recovery of entire settlements of past populations. It thus began to look beyond the mechanical gathering of isolated bits of material culture to the reconstruction of past communities, attempting to grasp the archaeological equivalent of the ecologists' group and the social anthropologist's organization-bearing unit. Outstanding among Americans who have furthered this new orientation are Robert J. Braidwood of the University of Chicago and Gordon R. Willey of Harvard University. Braidwood's major concern was the unravelling of the origins of cultivation and stockbreeding in the Near East, and the bearing of these developments on the later course of Near Eastern civilization, exemplified in his *The Near East and the Foundations for Civilization* (1952). Gordon R. Willey, interested in the development of culture in the western hemisphere, produced the strategic archaeological study marking the turning point in American archaeology, in his *Prehistoric Settlement Patterns in the Virú Valley, Peru* (1953). The cumulative impact of this work on students and colleagues has firmly established the culture ecological approach in American archaeological studies. It also laid the basis for the use of archaeological data in the systematic comparison of cultural sequences. This possibility is exemplified in Braidwood and Willey's recent collaborative effort *Courses Toward Urban Life* (1962), the product of a symposium to which scholars contributed papers on alternative patterns of development from food collecting to the establishment of urbanism in sixteen areas of the world.

At the same time, this change of perspective and technique also received strong influences from Europe. Especially important was the catalytic role of V. Gordon Childe (1892-1957), the British archaeologist, who in *Man Makes Himself* (1936) and *What Happened in History* (1946) formulated the transitions from food gathering to food production, from food production to urbanism, as a series of "revolutions," and analyzed the interrelationships between the primary civilizations in which the "urban" revolution first occurred to their barbarian hinterlands. Equally provocative and seminal in thinking about the relation of political power and agriculture was the work of the German historian Karl A. Wittfogel who in *Wirtschaft und Gesellschaft Chinas* (1931) had put forward the hypothesis that large-scale water control, such as irrigation or defense against floods, encouraged state construction and management of the strategic hydraulic complex, and hence implied a despotic centralization of power. Like many others, Wittfogel sought refuge from the political upheavals of prewar period in the United States, where he became director of the Chinese History Project at Columbia University. His major work in English, *Oriental Despotism: A Comparative Study of Total Power* (1957) restated his hydraulic thesis, and went on to grapple with the problem of whether and how methods of control developed in irrigation societies could be transmitted to societies with a different technological base. Also of importance was the work of the Mexican-Spanish archaeologist Pedro Armillas, now at Southern Illinois University, whose "paleosociological" interpretations of Middle American archaeological sequences influenced a generation of American archaeologists working in Mexico, beginning with his "A Sequence of Cultural Development in Meso-America," published in 1948.

These contributions have generated critics, as well as defenders and supporters. Undoubtedly some points of view, some interpretations, will not stand the test of evidence, and must yield to new points of view and new interpretations. The particular value of these efforts, however, lies not only in their novel arrangement of known sets of facts and in the discovery of new facts, but in their general effect on the direction of anthropological scholarship. They allow us to think more "ecologically," to grasp more completely the dynamic interplay of groups and cultures. They point toward a comparative morphology of complex cultural systems in terms of their underlying ecologies, their social organization and internal levels, their distribution of "core" and "marginal" areas, their internal and external symbiotic patterns, the constitution of their apparatus of power, their organizational strengths and limitations. They greatly sharpen our analytical sense for how social systems and cultures are put together.

Such a new understanding of the dynamic interplay of social groups and cultures will also yield a much more sophisticated picture of the symbolic systems of cultures than has been possible hitherto. The study of ideology and of religion has constituted a residual category for American anthropology. There has been a tendency to treat it either as the "expression" of some pattern general to the culture, or as a grab bag of miscellaneous items, ranging from ship-burial to the making of talismans. Just as American anthropology has been deficient in its ability to cope with social organization and the organization of power in a society, so it has been unable to see in religion the symbolic counterpart, the expression in symbolic terms, of organizational realities "on the ground." Here again, our British colleagues have made major contributions, whether we now think of Edward E. Evans-

Pritchard's study in his *Nuer Religion* (1956) of how the social organization of the Nuer operate in their religious life, or of Meyer Fortes' discussion, in his *Oedipus and Job in West African Religion* (1959), of the figures of Oedipus and Job as paradigms, respectively, of fate and supernatural justice, and his analysis of Tallensi religion in terms of the social genesis of these two principles. But, writing on this side of the Atlantic, Clifford Geertz recently made a similar major contribution to the study of symbolic systems, by projecting the symbolic code against the realities of social structure, in *The Religion of Java* (1960). In this work, he distinguishes between the peasant variant of Javanese religion, called abangan, the religious complex associated with the trader element, called santri, and the complex of the traditional elite, entitled prijaji. Abangan religion centers in the villages, and focuses upon performance of ritual feasts to dispel the disorder created by spirits and to reinstate equilibrium. Where abangan is ritual, santri is belief, codified by urban leaders and incarnated in a religious community of believers. Prijaji, on the other hand, represents the mystical striving for detached and effortless self-control, the ideal of a class of religio-aesthetically oriented warriors who seek polished perfection in etiquette, dance, shadow play, music, textile design, and language.

Although each of these aspects of Javanese religion points in a different direction, they are nevertheless complementary to each other. What are mystical practices for the prijaji are curing techniques on the peasant level. Prijaji banquets are abangan feasts. Where the prijaji interprets a shadow play as a battle between base passion and detached self-control, the abangan see but the manifest content of a fight between legendary heroes. The religious variants divide, but they also unite.

Where Geertz emphasized the structural dimensions of the Javenese symbol systems, others will stress the flow of symbolic communications. This approach derives, in large part, from the work of Robert Redfield. Redfield saw the city and the village, urban elite and rural folk, engaged in a continuous symbolic dialogue, a process of communication. While Redfield's original statements tended to be cast in bipolar terms, in terms of city and countryside, his approach proved applicable to the analysis of relations between any numbers of groups, and greatly gained in realism as a result. This was seen most clearly in recent research in India, where Redfield and others who have followed in his footsteps have applied it to the ordering of relations between the multifarious castes, villages, religions, sects, and traditions of this complex and heterogenous society. It has perhaps been most fruitful in application here because it is easier to view India as a vast network of communication channels embracing many different and differentiated units rather than in terms of the simpler contrasts between village and town, folk society and civil society, which served—crudely perhaps, but not inadequately—to deal with the simpler polarities of Occidental social structures.

In a joint article on "The Cultural Role of Cities" (written in 1954 and reprinted in Redfield's *Human Nature and the Study of Society*) Redfield and Milton Singer, his colleague at the University of Chicago, discussed the different functions of urban centers in regard to the accumulation of tradition, of systems of symbolic communication. Some centers, they saw, carried forward local patterns of custom and thought, while others imposed new patterns from the outside and strove to reshape local ways of life to new requirements. This weaving and reweaving of symbols and meanings is, in civilization, no longer the function of the occasional contemplative mind, but the specific task of groups of specialists, the professional thinkers and ritual agents of a complex society. In India, for example, these are usually the Brahman, though on occasion members of non-Brahman specialist castes of genealogists and mythographers may serve as well. As Malinowski had urged beginning ethnologists to "follow a woman home from the market place," to trace the connections of primitive life in terms of the movement and activities of actual persons engaged in their everyday tasks, so Redfield came to urge anthropologists to study these builders and mediators of symbolic communication, "the sweet-voiced singers on the temple steps."

To Redfield, the division between local mythology and universal doctrine, between peasant and philosopher or theologian, suggested a conceptual distinction between a "great" tradition and a "little" tradition, between the work of the reflective few and the unreflective many. This distinction evoked an image of "a wide band of great tradition linking —in reciprocal interaction—a great many local and popular traditions," and the researcher was encouraged to attempt to see the relationships between these traditions in the minutiae of village life. In 1955, McKim Mariott's "Little Communities in an Indigenous Civilization" reported, for example, an analysis of village festivals in the village of Kishan Gari in Uttar Pradesh. Mariott's study yielded new understandings of the ways in which the wider, pan-Indian Sanskrit tradition and the local ritual concepts and acts influenced each other:

the larger tradition covered the local with its elaborated rationale; the local tradition transformed the more universal tradition into closer fit with the demands of the local scene, in a process of "parochialization."

Where previous research into Indian religion and cosmology or sacred literature had focused almost exclusively on the study of sacred texts or artistic products, the understanding of these works could now be set in the enormously enriched context of larger "cultural performances" in which they received expression and life. Norvin Hein, who teaches Comparative Religion at Yale University, studied the dramas called Ram Lila, embodied in the story of the Ramayana, and contributed a paper on his findings to Milton Singer's *Traditional India* (1959). There he exhibits the complex interaction of the singer, who improvises from a seventeenth century vernacular adaptation of an ancient Sanskrit text, the actors, who dramatize portions of the reading, and the audience—all caught up in a performance that provides a ritual statement of the solidarity and continuity of Hindu culture. Such "cultural performances," exemplified further by weddings, temple festivals, dances, or musical performances, may be seen as constituting culturally standardized sequences of communication. Singer, who has elaborated this concept, comments in a 1955 article on "The Cultural Pattern of Indian Civilization" that "Indians, and perhaps all peoples, think of their culture as encapsulated in such discrete performances, which they can exhibit to outsiders as well as to themselves. For the outsider these can be conveniently taken as the most observable units of the cultural structure, for each cultural performance has a definitely limited time span, a beginning and an end, an organized program of activity, a set of per-

formers, an audience, and a place and occasion of performance."

Finally, one may study the changes in communication that
are crowding out the highly differentiated old media and
channels, emanating from many different centers and used
by different social networks in favor of more universal and
standardized channels that cut through this tangled web. In
"Changing Channels of Cultural Transmission in Indian
Civilization" (1959), McKim Mariott says: "Dominating
the new channels are a few metropolitan centers, nearly
identical culturally, having clear and separate jurisdiction.
Dominating each urban center are a few relatively centralized
institutions." The older transmitters and elaborators of tradition are bypassed in favor of the mass communication of
selected and standardized material.

But the possibilities of the approach go beyond the study
of communication in the field situation. It may be applied,
with productive results, to the great body of accumulated
folkloristic material, which hitherto the anthropologist has
hardly known how to utilize. Within the theoretical framework of social communication, we may now trace the routes
by which symbolic forms and complexes circulate between
city and country, between court and peasant village, between
"great" and "little" traditions. We may be enabled to see—in
more general and meaningful terms—the relation of peasant
dance to courtly pavane, of country dance and symphonic
elaboration, of baroque town house and peasant croft, of folk
ritual and myth and the "great" religions, of the folk legend
of Dr. Faustus to Goethe's *Faust,* of peasant tales first heard
at the knee of his nursemaid to Dostoevsky's *The Brothers
Karamazov.* Such studies may show us not only the inter-

connection of such forms, and the routes of transformation, but may differentiate for us also—in more general terms—the kinds of creativity open to the folk from the activities that require the existence of self-conscious "great" traditions elaborated by specialists. Not least, as Gordon R. Willey has pointed out, the concept of an art style as communication code will serve the archaeologist attempting to assign meaning to objects recovered from large contiguous zones that, though mute in themselves, bear the stigmata of similar ritual conceptions and practices embodied in common artistic form. With communication set more firmly in its social and cultural matrix, we shall also approach more meaningfully the problem of style, and the implied concepts of selection and habit channeling, without falling into the error of letting style refer mainly to the parts of culture that have an aesthetic or intellectual content and of ignoring the economic, political, moral, religious, and familial content. (See Meyer Shapiro's criticism of Kroeber's *Style and Civilization,* in *American Anthropologist,* LXI, 1959, 305.) A natural history of style is possible no less than a natural history of value; and it would allow us to close the gap between the study of concrete behavior and the more overarching concepts built up on the notion of art forms as a model of society.

There remains a final problem for the study of communication in complex sociocultural systems, one hardly touched upon by Redfield and yet important to their functioning: the study of the great collective social myths and master symbols that serve to draw large strata of the population toward collective goals. Here the anthropologist must join hands with the political scientist and the intellectual historian. What the anthropologist can contribute to such a study is not so much the definition of the elements contained in the myth, or a knowledge of their checkered histories, but a sense of where —in real life—the myth finds its points of reference, in what specific acts and problems the mythic elements lie anchored. This perspective is set forth in E. R. Leach's book on *Political Systems of Highland Burma: A Study of Kachin Social Structure* (1954): myth may be viewed much less as an intellectual precipitate of society than as an idiom in which given groups may communicate to each other both their unity and their disagreements. (For an example of this approach, see my article on "The Virgin of Guadalupe: A Mexican National Symbol," 1958.) How group speaks to group through similar idiomatic forms, in turn, has important bearing on how the society is articulated in discord as in consensus.

I have spoken of the transition from primitive culture to civilization as a problem for historical analysis, of how the investigation of parts of the civilizational process may be viewed systematically in relation to the process as a whole. Yet the transition from primitive to civilized entails still another dimension, to which anthropology must also address itself: the transformation implicit in this directional change of a shift in the relation between human means and human ends, in the nature of human experience in culture.

Among anthropologists, it was Edward Sapir who, in 1924, first explored the possibility that human experience in different cultures could vary *in value,* as a function of a qualitative variation in cultural organization. (Sapir's influential writings on this, as on many other topics, were gathered together in 1951 by David G. Mandelbaum of the University of California at Berkeley and edited in one volume as the *Selected Writings of Edward Sapir in Language, Culture, and*

Personality.) On this occasion Sapir attempted to approach the problem of qualitative variations among cultures by speaking of cultures as "genuine" and "spurious." Genuine culture was to him "inherently harmonious, balanced, self-satisfactory. It is the expression of a richly varied and yet somehow unified and consistent attitude toward life, an attitude which sees the significance of any one element of civilization in its relation to all others. It is, ideally speaking, a culture in which nothing is spiritually meaningless, in which no important part of the general functioning brings with it a sense of frustration, of misdirection or unsympathetic effort. It is not a spiritual hybrid of contradictory patches, of water-tight compartments of consciousness that avoids participation in a harmonious synthesis" (pp. 314-15). Such a culture, he said, "is internal, it works from the individual to ends" (p. 316). At a time when the concept of evolution was in general disrepute, Sapir gave voice to the possibility that such a culture could occur more easily among primitives than in modern society. "It is easier, generally speaking, for a genuine culture to subsist on a lower level of civilization; the differentiation of individuals as regards their social and economic functions is so much less than in the higher levels that there is less danger of the reduction of the individual to an unintelligible fragment of the social organism" (p. 318). In modern society, on the other hand, "the remoter ends tend to split off altogether from the immediate ones" (p. 319); "immediate ends cease to be felt as chief ends and gradually become necessary means, but only means, toward the attainment of the more remote ends" (p. 320). Thus, whereas in a "genuine" culture work is intimately connected with the whole web of activities, in our civilization ("spurious" by implication) "industrialism, as developed up to the present time . . . in harnessing machines to our uses . . . has not known how to avoid the harnessing of the majority of mankind to its machines" (p. 316). Sapir here comes close to the concept of alienation, as developed by the young Karl Marx and taken up, in one form or another, by modern existentialism in the postwar period. "The American Indian who solves the economic problem with salmon-spear and rabbit-snare operates on a relatively low level of civilization, but he represents an incomparably higher solution than our telephone girl of the questions that culture has to ask of economics." Why? "The Indian's salmon-spearing is a culturally higher type of activity than that of telephone girl or mill hand simply because there is normally no sense of spiritual frustration during its prosecution, no feeling of subservience to tyrannous yet largely inchoate demands, because it works naturally with all the rest of the Indian's activities instead of standing out as a desert patch of merely economic effort in the whole of life" (p. 316). Since we cannot return to salmon-spear and rabbit-snare, what is Sapir's solution? We are condemned to lead fragmented existences, but the individual may learn how to "compensate himself out of the non-economic, the non-utilitarian spheres—social, religious, scientific, aesthetic" (p. 319). This posing of the problem is but an earlier form of the modern question of how men are to use their leisure time now that the machine has proved capable of satisfying a large percentage of our wants, demanding only simple operations to keep it charged and running.

We may note in Sapir's statements an overvaluation of primitive life, and an accompanying undervaluation of the immense effort and attendant boredom involved in scraping a bare living from an inhospitable world. No one who has seen the film *The Hunters,* depicting the struggle of four Bushmen to run to ground one badly wounded giraffe so as to provide food for themselves and their hungry families, can wholeheartedly support Sapir's statement. There is no gainsaying the primitive's lack of technological control, his narrow margin of safety, his easy exposure to hunger and disease. Nor does Sapir pay sufficient attention to the insecurities that may, on occasion, drive a hard-pressed people to build a tightly organized and coordinated culture to serve as a shield against external pressures. Highly coherent cultures, such as, for instance, those of the Zuñi and Hopi have been shown to pay a high price for their holism. (See Esther S. Goldfrank's "Socialization, Personality, and the Structure of Pueblo Society," 1945.) And yet we may agree that Sapir's remarks touch on a problem to which anthropology has yet to address itself with both objectivity and compassion.

Sapir's conceptual distinction found few admitted followers; anthropologists probably bridled at its subjectivism. One may discern its influence in the works of Ruth Benedict, whose discussion of highly patterned cultures bears some resemblance to Sapir's idea of genuine cultures. But if such a link existed between Sapir's formulations and her own, that link was never rendered explicit in her writings. In a paper published in the *American Anthropologist,* XLIV (1942), Robert Zingg applied the notion of "spurious culture" to the Mexican Tarahumara, who—though primitive enough— live atomistic lives, highly charged with hostility and fear, in the inhospitable reaches of Chihuahua and Durango. Melvin Tumin also made use of Sapir's concepts to describe the difference between Indians and non-Indians in San Luis Jilotepeque, in eastern Guatemala. Tumin's article "Culture, Genuine and Spurious: A Reevaluation" (1945) draws a contrast often noted before or since between the strongly community-oriented Indians, who adjust to the world in which they must live with an acceptance bred of passivity, and the non-Indian ladinos, who strive against each other in competition and occasional violence to reach their place on the national scene, a much larger arena than that provided by the small highland village. But these contributions, interesting as they are in their own rights, remained mere glosses upon Sapir's basic text, until Robert Redfield posed the problem in a different way, from a different direction.

Redfield drew upon Durkheim and Maine for his theoretical inspiration, but applied some of their formulations to the field study of Mexican communities in *The Folk Culture of Yucatan* (1941). He, too, cast his statements in terms of a conceptual polarity, opposing the ways of the folk to the ways of the city; he saw the folkways located in a characteristic folk culture, city ways in urban culture. The folk society was seen as isolated and culturally homogeneous; as a result its ways of life were strongly cohesive and consistent with one another, embued with sacredness, and productive of a strong sense of collective solidarity. Urban society could be considered animated by the opposite qualities: intensity of contact of all kinds; heterogeneity; lack of organization among its many ways of life; individualization; secularization—with people "ceasing to believe because they cease to understand," and ceasing "to understand because they cease to do the things that express the understandings" (p. 364). This also produces a change in essential moral qualities. In *The Primitive World and Its Transformation* (1953), Redfield analyzed this moral transformation in terms of a polarity taken over from the sociologists C. H. Cooley and Robert E. Park, the polarity between the "moral order" and the "technical order." The moral order referred to shared convictions "as to what is thought to be inherently, morally, right." He saw precivilized society as dominated by such shared convictions of right. In contrast, the technical order is seen as "that order which results from mutual usefulness, from deliberate coercion, or from the mere utilization of the same means. In the technical order men are bound by things, or are themselves things. They are organized by necessity or expediency" (p. 21). "In the folk society the moral order is great and the technical order is small" (p.23); "the moral order predominates over the technical order" (p. 24). In civilization, however, the growth of the technical order outstrips the development of the moral order, to the extent that one may speak of a culture lag between the movement of the two orders (p. 74). Here Redfield, perhaps unknowingly, came to echo Sapir.

One may take issue with the formulation, and yet grant it a measure of validity. Abraham Edel, writing on "Some Relations of Philosophy and Anthropology" in 1953, pointed out, for instance, that what Redfield calls the technical order, in opposition to the moral order, is really also a moral order of a special kind, a Benthamite kind of moral order. One may go further, and say, as Redfield himself did, that civilization "is creator to the moral order as well as destroyer" of a moral order that disapproves of hunger and disease and employs its knowledge to banish these twin scourges of mankind, of a moral order that allows us to banish the dangers of subjective personal projections and face the threat of randomness through the application of science and probability calculations. As Kroeber realized, civilization renders obsolete the "infantile obsession" with human physiological events, the bizarre behavior of the shaman, the beckoning of the diviner. We have figuratively cut the umbilical cord that ties us to nature, and we need no longer seek supernatural significance in the symptoms of the mentally unbalanced. Moreover, as Redfield himself pointed out, civilization bursts the narrow parochialism of the folk that sees only itself as human, and regards the stranger as inhuman, to produce a new universal conception of humanity embracing all men alike. The moral problem of civilization is thus perhaps not phrased correctly as a lag between technical order and moral order; it lies rather in the paradox that would grant universal humanity to all men, only to treat all men as things.

As Stanley Diamond, anthropologist at the National Institute of Mental Health, has noted in his *The Search for the Primitive* (1963), "delineated" individuals can develop more easily in primitive society than in civilized society. Lacking the individualized economic base of modern society and the monopolistic exercise of organized force, primitive societies produce no anxieties about the right to work "as a peer among peers," nor the alienation involved in accepting the dictates of impersonal and arbitrary authority. Slow to change, such societies produce little tension in the individual; holistic, in Sapir's sense, they promote meaningful individual participation. In primitive society, a person is a person in a community of kinsmen, among others like himself. Modes of thought are similarly concrete, tied to the individual event as ultimate reality. To cope with the inevitable anxieties of life at critical times, such societies possess great rituals in which individual and group can experience catharsis and express creativity. We possess what primitives lack—technology, science, rationality —but our tendency to abstraction, our impersonality, our tendency to aggregate people for technical ends, are all tending to destroy for us, in Diamond's words, "the immediate and ramifying sense of the person."

Again, one is struck by an overvaluation of the primitive. It is one thing to grow to adulthood in a tightly organized community, quite another to be an adult in it. The presence of kinsmen may be warm and satisfying; it may also be cloying and charged negatively with the endless demands, the unfulfilled and unfulfillable exigencies, of kinship. Great rituals may be cathartic and creative; they can also be repetitive, monotonous, and mechanical. Nevertheless, here too one discerns a problem, the problem of defining the kind of person produced by primitive culture, and its necessary problematic complement, the kind of person demanded by civilization.

Does civilization, more than primitive culture, render the segments of life experience discontinuous, thus molding persons who can easily adapt their personalities to meet new demands? Does civilization require that the individual cope with a wider range of inconsistencies, and thus favor individuals who can with greater calm combine various kinds of inconsistent behavior and who can bear with greater fortitude the tension of greater intellectual heterogeneity? Does civilization confront the individual with a quantitatively and qualitatively vaster store of objectified experience, and hence repress more completely individual subjective experience? Does civilization substitute more readily collective cognition, produced by a complex division of labor, for personal wisdom, but also turn the *folie à seul* or *à deux* more easily into the folly of the multitude? These questions are raised here not to

85

furnish easy answers, but to remind anthropologists to participate in their solution. They can, moreover, be answered oper-
ationally. If they were posed first by men strongly involved
with presuppositions of value, there is no reason why anthropology cannot address itself to the task of ascertaining what
kind of person is *probable* and *possible* within the framework
of a given social order. We shall then be able also to assess
more concretely and meaningfully what has been gained, and
what lost, in the course of human development.

EPILOGUE

I have examined, in these pages, anthropology at its most general, as a discipline concerned with man and the nature of his unfolding. I have inevitably slighted the contributions that have dealt, faithfully and patiently, with man in all his particularity. But I have done so in the twin hope of showing what sort of image of man emerges from the endeavors of modern anthropology, and how anthropology has contributed to man's understanding of himself. Anthropologists are apt to be modest about the possibilities of their discipline, to discuss the wider implications of their knowledge with diffidence. Yet, in our time, such timidities enshrine a danger, the danger of separation between private faith in science and public defense of that faith, of a divorce between vision and act, to the detriment of the vision that can alone justify the act. In a complex and complicated world, there is comfort in collecting ever more bits of pottery, ever more refined observations of behavior, ever more sophisticated tallies of blood group distributions, as if the deposition of ever larger middens of "hard data" were sufficient justification in itself. At the very worst, this can degenerate into a narrow empiricism that is both sterile and cowardly. It is cowardly because it begs the questions of meaning and significance. It is sterile because the depositories of facts can be quickened into life only by exercise of the imagination. This essay, then, should be read as an exercise of the anthropological imagination.

I began this essay with some thoughts on the relation of anthropology to the humanities. We have seen that the relation is not easily defined, since anthropology is, as I have said, less subject matter than a bond between subject matters. It is in part history, part literature; in part natural science, part social science; it strives to study men both from within and from without; it represents both a manner of looking at man and a vision of man—"the most scientific of the humanities, the most humanist of the sciences." In an age of increased specialization, it strives to be above specialties, to connect and to articulate them. Anthropology is probably not alone in this. If its endeavors seem to contradict prevailing trends, the contradiction is more apparent than real; the very process of specialization continuously spawns new subfields along and across the boundaries of the established disciplines. Thus, the recent past, for example, has seen the growth of ecology, ethology, and communication science, with which, in fact, anthropology has much in common; like these fields, anthropology thrives on the very heterogeneity of its subject matter. And, like other fields, it thrives on its peculiar combination of its interest in particular cases with a most general perspective on the course of human development. For it is certainly an unusual reliance on the particular that sets off the anthropological approach from other social scientific endeavors. Essentially, the anthropological position is that one must first view events in all their richness and texture before one can be confident of having selected the appropriate variables for analysis. The social scientist is, in general, more "tough-minded." He approaches reality with a hypothesis that—like an X ray—reveals anatomical detail in sharp relief against the contextual ground. He then proceeds to grasp reality sharply with the forceps of the mind, and to dissect it without loss of blood upon the operating table of his analysis. The anthropologist, too, has presuppositions, prejudices, sensitivities; he, too, must view reality through his personal lens. But—more romantically inclined perhaps than his other social scientific colleagues—he distrusts the capacity of his reason to achieve sharply delineated conceptual forms that can be imposed on the material a priori. He cannot bring himself to sever detail and context in cleanly fashion; he plays his presuppositions as hunches, disciplining himself to let reality invade and disturb him. Like the psychotherapist, he acts upon the premise that what seems most obvious, most clear-cut, and most readily apparent in a situation may turn out to be most complicated, and least evident; and he watches for tell-tale signs that will betray this complexity and reveal its true significance to those who have waited patiently and without mechanical prejudgments.

Hence, the anthropologist will always pay tribute to true skill in observing detail and eliciting meaning. There is a sense in which, in the private ranking systems of American anthropologists, the first-class recorder of ethnographic detail ranks more highly than the most gifted theorist. Just as the historian will always take delight in reconstructions that evoke *wie es eigentlich gewesen,* so the anthropologist will always relish expert descriptions of Hanunoo betel chewing, of the use of indigenous weights and measures in a Haitian market, of children as errand runners in a Mexican Indian community.

In this emphasis on the particular—indeed, on the characteristics of the individual case as an ultimate touchstone against which theory must be tested—anthropology resembles literature. For literature, too, focuses on the particular as *ultima ratio*. Good literature is not written by constructing frames of universal applicability; these frames must first be filled with the vibrancy of particular life, *in order to* become universally meaningful. So anthropology, too, seeks this vibrancy of particular life. Nevertheless, it differs basically from literature, and this not only because its heroes are collective heroes, as in *Solomon Island Society, We the Tikopia,* and *The People of Alor.* Literature, likewise, can portray collective heroes, even if it must do so through the portrayal of individualized men, as—for instance—in André Malraux's *Man's Fate* or *Man's Hope,* or Lawrence Durrell's *Alexandria Quartet.* The writer, however, creates his work of art; the anthropologist, to the contrary, describes and analyzes a phenomenon he has done nothing to create. The work of art with which the anthropologist is concerned exists when he comes to it—it is the culture wrought by Siuai or Tikopia or the people of Atimelang—all he can do is capture the phenomenon with fidelity and insight.

Nor can the anthropologist be content with "fixing" a particular case in the pages of his notebook. He must go on to contrast and compare it with other cases, to construct generalizations and theories, to narrow the play of possibilities. It is clear that we shall never have "completely" open minds; it is likely that we should not want them. Only computers have completely open minds, and they must be put to work by minds that know what they want. Nevertheless, we require minds that can make the most of the experience of the unfamiliar—of what anthropologists call culture shock—to repattern their habitual neural pathways. (See, for a not-so-fictionalized and truly excellent account of this experience,

Eleanor Smith Bowen's *Return to Laughter,* 1954). One may remark upon the resemblance of this process to what Anthony Wallace has called "mazeway reintegration." He referred to the repatterning and reshaping of cognitive patterns in the course of religious and other movements that attempted to revitalize a culture heavily exposed to the hazards of cultural change. It may not be amiss to speculate in similar terms on the value of this experience to anthropologists, as on their quasi-religious attachment to their profession. Whatever the psychological aspects of this will to flexibility, however, there can be no doubt that it is the indispensable prerequisite of good fieldwork. And, as long as anthropologists do fieldwork, therefore, it will constitute a countervailing force to the drive for generalization.

This particularism has, I believe, two virtues that are important in our times. We live in a period in which the involvement and mobilization of large numbers of men in both peace and war increasingly require us to think in large numbers, whether we are attempting to measure the gross national income, the actual or potential effects of automation, or the thermal and fire aftermath of nuclear detonations. Large-scale phenomena produce intellectual responses endeavoring to grasp global problems in global terms. Such generalizing efforts are, however, all too often unidirectional—that is, they proceed from general suppositions and models to statistical statements that discount the individual case, or "average" it into oblivion. A statement that the annual per capita income in Greece is close to $200 is no use to Ioannis Tregaskis who made not $180 but $50, but whose income deficiencies have here been averaged out to obtain an operating model of a useful but fictitious average Greek. Here the anthropologist comes into his own. For he can set his data, obtained from flesh and blood informants in a local setting, against the more general measurements, garnered and aimed at a higher level, and thus provide a further test of their validity. Yet in doing this, he also does more.

In a true humanistic sense, an individual life, or even the sum of lives interlaced in a common fate, are entities irreducible to general statements. Of this men have long been aware. No account of Californian Indians brought to bay and destroyed has the reality of Theodora Kroeber's *Ishi in Two Worlds,* the story of Ishi, the last of the Yahi, just as no general account of persecution and human suffering has the immediate impact of *The Diary of Anne Frank,* or of Miguel del Castillo's *Child of Our Time.* In his particularism, the anthropologist therefore raises again, in a different form, Dostoevsky's burning question of how to justify the good society that depends for its successful establishment upon the murder of a single child. It is in this spirit that Oscar Lewis in his *Children of Sánchez,* the cumulative autobiographies of a lower-class family living in a Mexico City slum, calls the anthropologist both "student and spokesman" of the poor who cannot speak for themselves. Nor need such an emphasis be confined to the study of individuals. Hortense Powdermaker's recent study of Luanshya in Northern Rhodesia, views with scientific rigor and compassion "the human situation on the Rhodesian copperbelt."

The second virtue of anthropology in this time of global decisions and macro-analysis is implicit in the first. Where the generalizing scientist all too often perceives only variables, yielding abstract correlations at better than 0.05 level of probability, the anthropologist retains a strong sense for the interrelationships of cultural events, for the "network" of social relations, for the "fabric" of human culture. This is sometimes expressed by saying that the anthropologist is "holistic" in his approach. The word is perhaps unfortunate because it seems to commit the anthropologist to a philosophical approach that implies more than he would be willing to grant. But it does point to the characteristic quest of the anthropologist, which is to study the life of a group in its multiple interrelationships, to discern the economic in the religious, the political in the social, the social in the economic. Clearly, social and cultural life is lived not in compartments, but integrally, and the anthropologist seeks to grasp what integration he can perceive. He realizes that it is this integration that meets the needs of a people, as it also guides their needs; and he is aware of the adaptive qualities of these links, their resistances to change, the wider ramifications in the lives of people when they are broken. Hence, where observers who view the microcosm only from the top of the social pyramid see only aggregates and numbers, he, taking the mole's-eye view, perceives microcosmic systems, relationships below the threshold of superficial observation.

From anthropologists, we learn why an improved pumping device for irrigation water failed to take hold in an Indian village despite its clear superiority over existing means of accomplishing the same end: because its introduction would have required greater changes in land tenure, settlement pattern, and neighborly relationships than people were willing to envisage. (See McKim Mariott's "Technological Change in Overdeveloped Rural Areas," 1952.) We learn how the introduction of steel axes among the Yir Yoront of Australia changed not only their relation to the mission stations that acted as main sources of supply, but upset relations between men and women, young and old, as well as undermining the ideological system of totemic loyalties. (See Lauriston Sharp's "Steel Axes for Stone Age Australians," 1952.) We learn how the impact of weekend tourism on a village in Jalisco, Mexico, not only brought new sources of wealth, but also increased sales of land, and conflicts over sales of land, introduced new means of policing the village to guarantee the safety of the visitors, brought on limitations on the carrying of weapons, changed the local power structure, and increased aggression that is finding outlets through substitute channels. (See Theron A. Nuñez's "Tourism, Tradition and Acculturation: *Weekendismo* in a Mexican Village," 1963.)

Apparently trivial in themselves, such microscopic shifts seem to effect the larger society but little. Yet from rivulets large rivers flow, of many such microscopic shifts great events are born, and the trivial disturbances of yesterday may herald the social upheaval of tomorrow.

But in these pages I have also claimed for anthropology both a greater opportunity and a greater obligation: the creation of an image of man that will be adequate to the experience of our time.

If anthropology has been defined as a science of man, then a science of man it must be, or perish. For the first time in the history of anthropology, as in the development of human thought about man, we stand upon the threshold of a scientifically informed conception of the human career as a universal process. It differs from previous formulations in its understanding that the universal human process is not unitary, but an articulation of many diverse parts and forces, which are yet interconnected and directional. This process is material and materially demonstrable; it owes its diagnostic features to the characteristics of the human design, which can achieve pattern and shape only through determinate cultures. The unity of man is due neither to an ultimate biological homunculus inherent in each man, driving events in the same biologically determined direction, nor to a unitary process located in the mind of God. It is a process of the involvement of man with man, through the medium of human culture.

For the first time in human history, we have transcended the inherited divisions of the human phenomenon into segments of time and segments of space. Our consciousness now embraces not only Paris and London, Moscow and Peking, but also Teotihuacan, Chan-Chan, Lasah, Niniveh; not only French and Vietnamese, Bolivians and Greeks, but also Navaho, Nentsi, Wulemba, Wiyot. Nor is it meaningful any longer, except for the sake of momentary convenience, to think in terms of single unitary models of men, be they the model of Economic Man, or Man in the Skinner Box, or Man cast out of paradise and laboring in the throes of original guilt. This is in no way to gainsay the temporary and limited utility of drawing a bead on one solitary aspect of the human phenomenon as long as we remain aware that no one stationary perspective will any longer exhaust the possibilities of man. We have left behind, once and for all, the paleotechnic age of the grounded observer who can draw only one line of sight between the object and himself. We have entered the physical and the intellectual space age, and we are now in a position to circumnavigate man, to take our readings from any point in both space and time.

I shall state here my belief that it is the task of anthropology to assert this possibility of a true science of man. We all know that this embryonic science of man is in danger, just as man himself is in danger. The future of anthropology and anthropologists is no more, nor less, assured than that of other men. Man may succeed, or he may not: indeed, victory may be as costly as defeat. Yet the logic of the anthropological position is unequivocal, whether or not anthropologists live up to its implications. We have asserted and demonstrated the unity of man in the articulation of the cultural process; to deny these links with our past and present is to put blinders on our vision, to retreat to a narrower adaptation, to turn our backs on what we may yet become. In describing and analyzing the cultural process, we have asserted the autonomy of science: we have taken our stand beyond—above—existing cultures. If one asks where this point of vantage is located in real time and space, the answer is clear: the anthropological point of vantage is that of a world culture, struggling to be born. As a scientist, the anthropologist both represents its embryonic possibilities and works to create it. If that culture fails, so will anthropology. Finally, we have asserted that what is worth studying is human experience; not economic experience, not psychological experience, not religious experience, cut into segments and studied separately, but human experience understood as the experience of life. This I believe to be an assertion of freedom against slavery. For each segmentary model of man is also a straitjacket for men. The economist utilizing a segmented model of Economic Man not only describes men as economic men; he also tells them to be economic men. The psychologist studying man as a set of responses, triggered by appropriate stimuli, teaches his subjects to act as the experiment demands. These schemes have simplicity to commend them, and it may be that we shall recast men in their image, to increase predictability and orderliness in human society. But the anthropologist, who has had occasion to confront the range of human possibilities, is committed also to an image of man that asserts both the variability and complexity of human life.

If I am right, then in the process of creating that science of man that will underwrite the new world culture and its new possibilities, anthropology will also change itself, and change itself beyond recognition. Some of these changes are already under way. To make them possible, in a world of necessity, is our obligation.

BIBLIOGRAPHY

Aberle, David F., "The Influence of Linguistics on Early Culture and Personality Theory" in *Essays in the Science of Culture: In Honor of Leslie A. White,* ed. Gertrude E. Dole and Robert L. Carneiro. New York: Thomas Y. Crowell Company, 1960.

Armillas, Pedro, "A Sequence of Cultural Development in Meso-America" in *A Reappraisal of Peruvian Archaeology,* ed. Wendell C. Bennett. Memoirs of the Society for American Archaeology, No. 4. Menasha, Wis.: Society for American Archaeology, 1948.

Baldwin, Leland Dewitt, *God's Englishman: The Evolution of the Anglo-Saxon Spirit.* Boston: Little, Brown & Co., 1944.

Benedict, Ruth F., *Patterns of Culture.* Boston: Houghton Mifflin Company, 1934.

———, *The Chrysanthemum and the Sword: Patterns of Japanese Culture.* Boston: Houghton Mifflin Company, 1946.

Berger, Bennett M., "The Myth of Suburbia," *Journal of Social Issues,* XVII (1961), 38-49.

Bowen, Eleanor Smith, *Return to Laughter.* New York: Harper & Row, Publishers, 1954.

Braidwood, Robert J., *The Near East and the Foundations for Civilization.* Eugene: University of Oregon Press, 1952.

———, and Gordon R. Willey, *Courses Toward Urban Life: Archaeological Considerations of Some Cultural Alternates.* Viking Fund Publications in Anthropology, No. 32. Chicago: Aldine Publishing Co., 1962.

Bruner, Jerome S., "Myth and Identity" in *Myth and Mythmaking,* ed. Henry A. Murray. New York: George Braziller, Inc., 1960.

Bunzel, Ruth, *The Pueblo Potter: A Study of Creative Imagination in Primitive Art*. Columbia University Contributions to Anthropology, Vol. 8. New York: Columbia University Press, 1929.

Childe, V. Gordon, *Man Makes Himself*. London: C. A. Watts & Co., Ltd., 1936.

————, *What Happened in History*. New York: Pelican Books, 1946.

Devereux, George, "Art and Mythology: A General Theory" in *Studying Personality Cross-Culturally*, ed. Bert Kaplan. New York: Harper & Row, Publishers, 1961.

Diamond, Stanley, "The Search for the Primitive" in *Man's Image in Medicine and Anthropology*, ed. Iago Galdston. Institute of Social and Historical Medicine, New York Academy of Science, Monograph IV. New York: International Universities Press, 1963.

Dodds, Eric R., *The Greeks and the Irrational*. Berkeley: University of California Press, 1951.

Dundes, Alan, "Earth-Diver: Creation of the Mythopoeic Male," *American Anthropologist*, LXIV (1962), 1032-51.

Edel, Abraham, "Some Relations of Philosophy and Anthropology," *American Anthropologist*, LV (1953), 649-60.

————, "Anthropology and Ethics in Common Focus," *Journal of the Royal Anthropological Institute*, XCII (1962), 55-72.

Eggan, Dorothy, "Dream Analysis" in *Studying Personality Cross-Culturally*, ed. Bert Kaplan. New York: Harper & Row, Publishers, 1961.

Eggan, Fred, *Social Organization of the Western Pueblos*. Chicago: University of Chicago Press, 1950.

Elias, Norbert, *Ueber den Prozess der Zivilisation*, 2 vols. Basel: Verlag Haus Zum Falken, 1939.

Elmendorf, W. W., and Alfred L. Kroeber, *The Structure of Twana Culture with Comparative Notes on the Structure of Yurok Culture*. Research Studies, a Quarterly Publication of Washington State University, Vol. 28, No. 3, Monograph Supplement No. 2. Pullman: Washington State University, 1960.

Evans-Pritchard, Edward E., *Nuer Religion.* Oxford: Clarendon Press, 1956.

Fairchild, Hoxie N., *The Noble Savage: A Study in Romantic Naturalism.* New York: Columbia University Press, 1928.

Finley, Moses I., *The World of Odysseus.* New York: The Viking Press, Inc., 1954.

Fortes, Meyer, *Oedipus and Job in West African Religion.* London: Cambridge University Press, 1959.

Geertz, Clifford, *The Religion of Java.* New York: Free Press of Glencoe, Inc., 1960.

Gerbrands, A. A., *Art as an Element of Culture, Especially in Negro Africa.* Medelingen van het Rijksmuseum voor Volkenkunde, Leiden, No. 12. Leiden: E. J. Brill, 1957.

Goffman, Erving, "The Nature of Deference and Demeanor," *American Anthropologist,* LVIII (1956), 473-502.

Goldfrank, Esther S., "Socialization, Personality, and the Structure of Pueblo Society." *American Anthropologist,* XLVII (1945), 516-39.

Hallowell, A. Irving, "Personality Structure and the Evolution of Man," *American Anthropologist,* LII (1950), 159-73.

Hein, Norvin, "The Rām Līlā" in *Traditional India: Structure and Change,* ed. Milton Singer. Bibliographical and Special Series, Vol. 10. Philadelphia: American Folklore Society, 1959.

Hymes, Dell H., "The Ethnography of Speaking" in *Anthropology and Human Behavior,* ed. Thomas Gladwin and William Sturtevant. Washington, D.C.: Anthropological Society of Washington, 1962.

Jones, William T., *The Romantic Syndrome: Toward a New Method in Cultural Anthropology and History of Ideas.* The Hague: Martinus Nijhoff, 1961.

Kaplan, Bert, *A Study of Rorschach Responses in Four Cultures*. Papers of the Peabody Museum of American Archaeology and Ethnology, Harvard University, Vol. 42, No. 2, 1954.

Kluckhohn, Clyde K. M., "Toward a Comparison of Value-Emphases in Different Cultures" in *The State of the Social Sciences,* ed. Leonard White. Chicago: University of Chicago Press, 1956.

————, "Recurrent Themes in Myths and Mythmaking" in *Myth and Mythmaking,* ed. Henry A. Murray. New York: George Braziller, Inc., 1960.

————, *Anthropology and the Classics* (The Colver Lectures). Providence: Brown University Press, 1961.

————, and William Morgan, "Some Notes on Navaho Dreams" in *Psychoanalysis and Culture: Essays in Honor of Géza Róheim,* ed. George B. Wilbur and Warner Muensterberger. New York: International Universities Press, 1956.

Kluckhohn, Florence R., and Fred L. Strodtbeck, *Variations in Value Orientations*. New York: Harper & Row, Publishers, 1961.

Kroeber, Alfred L., *Cultural and Natural Areas of Native North America*. University of California Publications in American Archaeology and Ethnology, XXXVIII (1939). Berkeley: University of California Press.

————, *The Nature of Culture*. Chicago: University of Chicago Press, 1952.

————, "History of Anthropological Thought" in *Yearbook of Anthropology, 1955,* ed. William L. Thomas Jr. New York: Wenner-Gren Foundation for Anthropological Research, 1955.

————, *A Roster of Civilizations and Culture*. Viking Fund Publications in Anthropology, No. 33. Chicago: Aldine Publishing Co., 1962.

Kroeber, Theodora, *Ishi in Two Worlds*. Berkeley: University of California Press, 1961.

Leach, E. R., *Political Systems of Highland Burma: A Study of Kachin Social Structure.* Cambridge: Harvard University Press, 1954.

Lévi-Strauss, Claude, *Les Structures élémentaires de la parenté.* Paris: Presses Universitaires de France, 1949.

———, *Anthropologie structurale.* Paris: Librairie Plon, 1958. (*Structural Anthropology,* trans. Claire Jacobson and Brooke Grundfest Schoepf. Boston: Beacon Press, Inc., 1963.)

———, *Le Totémisme aujourd'hui.* Paris: Presses Universitaires de France, 1962. (*Totemism,* trans. Rodney Needham. Boston: Beacon Press, Inc., 1963.)

Lewis, Oscar, *The Children of Sánchez: Autobiography of a Mexican Family.* New York: Random House, 1961.

Livingstone, Frank B., "Anthropological Implications of Sickle Cell Gene Distribution in West Africa," *American Anthropologist,* LX (1958), 533-62.

Malinowski, Bronislaw, *Argonauts of the Western Pacific.* New York: E. P. Dutton & Co., Inc., 1922.

———, *Sex and Repression in Savage Society.* New York: Harcourt, Brace & World, Inc., 1927.

Mandelbaum, David G., ed., *Selected Writings of Edward Sapir in Language, Culture, and Personality.* Berkeley: University of California Press, 1951.

Mariott, McKim, "Technological Change in Overdeveloped Rural Areas," *Economic Development and Cultural Change,* I (1952), 261-72.

———, "Little Communities in an Indigenous Civilization" in *Village India: Studies in the Little Community,* ed. McKim Mariott. Comparative Studies of Cultures and Civilizations, No. 6. Chicago: University of Chicago Press, 1955.

———, "Changing Channels of Cultural Transmission in Indian Civilization" in *Intermediate Societies, Social Mobility and Communication,* ed. Verne F. Ray. Proceedings of the 1959 Annual Spring Meeting of the American Ethnological Society.

Mead, Margaret, *Coming of Age in Samoa.* New York: William Morrow & Co., Inc., 1928.

————, *Sex and Temperament in Three Primitive Societies.* New York: William Morrow & Co., Inc., 1935.

————, *Male and Female.* New York: William Morrow & Co., Inc., 1955.

————, *An Anthropologist at Work: Writings of Ruth Benedict.* Boston: Houghton Mifflin Company, 1959.

————, "Retrospects and Prospects" in *Anthropology and Human Behavior,* ed. Thomas Gladwin and William Sturtevant. Washington, D.C.: Anthropological Society of Washington, 1962.

Mering, Otto von, *A Grammar of Human Values.* Pittsburgh: University of Pittsburgh Press, 1961.

Mills, George T., *Navaho Art and Culture.* Colorado Springs: Taylor Museum of the Colorado Fine Arts Center, 1959.

Nuñez, Theron A., "Tourism, Tradition and Acculturation: *Weekendismo* in a Mexican Village," *Ethnology,* II (1962), 347-52.

Ostwald, Wilhelm, "The Modern Theory of Energetics," *The Monist,* XVII (1907), 481-515.

Powdermaker, Hortense, *Copper Town: Changing Africa. The Human Situation on the Rhodesian Copperbelt.* New York: Harper & Row, Publishers, 1962.

Radcliffe-Brown, Alfred R., *The Andaman Islanders.* London: Cambridge University Press, 1922.

————, *A Natural Science of Society.* New York: Free Press of Glencoe, Inc., 1957.

Redfield, Margaret Park, ed., *Human Nature and the Study of Society: The Papers of Robert Redfield,* Vol. 1. Chicago: University of Chicago Press, 1962.

Redfield, Robert, *The Folk Culture of Yucatan.* Chicago: University of Chicago Press, 1941.

————, *The Primitive World and Its Transformation.* Ithaca: Cornell University Press, 1953.

————, *The Little Community: Viewpoints for the Study of a Human Whole.* Chicago: University of Chicago Press, 1955.

Róheim, Géza, *The Origin and Function of Culture.* Nervous and Mental Disease Monographs, No. 69. New York: Nervous and Mental Disease Publishing Company, 1943.

Sahlins, Marshall D., *Social Stratification in Polynesia.* Seattle: University of Washington Press, 1958.

————, and Elman R. Service, *Evolution and Culture.* Ann Arbor: University of Michigan Press, 1960.

Shapiro, Meyer, Review of A. L. Kroeber's *Style and Civilization* in *American Anthropologist,* LXI (1959), 303-05.

Sharp, Lauriston, "Steel Axes for Stone Age Australians" in *Human Problems in Technological Change: A Casebook,* ed. Edward H. Spicer. New York: Russell Sage Foundation, 1952.

Singer, Milton, "The Cultural Pattern of Indian Civilization: A Preliminary Report of a Methodological Field Study," *Far Eastern Quarterly,* XV (1955), 223-36.

Spencer, Robert F., "The Humanities in Cultural Anthropology" in *Method and Perspective in Anthropology: Papers in Honor of Wilson D. Wallis,* ed. Robert F. Spencer. Minneapolis: University of Minnesota Press, 1954.

Spuhler, James N., ed., *The Evolution of Man's Capacity for Culture.* Detroit: Wayne State University Press, 1959.

Steward, Julian H., *Basin-plateau Aboriginal Sociopolitical Groups.* Bureau of American Ethnology, Bulletin 120. Washington, D.C.: U.S. Government Printing Office, 1938.

————, ed., *Handbook of South American Indians,* 7 vols. Bureau of American Ethnology, Bulletin 143. Washington, D.C.: U.S. Government Printing Office, 1946-59.

————, *Theory of Culture Change: The Methodology of Multilinear Evolution.* Urbana: University of Illinois Press, 1955.

Tumin, Melvin, "Culture, Genuine and Spurious: A Reevaluation," *American Sociological Review,* X (1945), 199-207.

Vogt, Evon Z., "On the Concepts of Structure and Process in Cultural Anthropology," *American Anthropologist,* LXII (1960), 18-33.

Wallace, Anthony, "A Possible Technique for Recognizing Psychological Characteristics of the Ancient Maya from an Analysis of Their Art," *American Image,* VII (1950), 239-58.

———, "Mazeway Resynthesis: A Biocultural Theory of Religious Inspiration" in *Transactions of the New York Academy of Sciences,* Vol. 18, Series 11 (1956), pp. 626-38.

———, *Culture and Personality.* Studies in Anthropology, No. 1. New York: Random House, 1961.

———, "The Psychic Unity of Human Groups," in *Studying Personality Cross-Culturally,* ed. Bert Kaplan. New York: Harper & Row, Publishers, 1961.

Washburn, Sherwood L., ed., *Social Life of Early Man.* Viking Fund Publications in Anthropology, No. 31. Chicago: Aldine Publishing Co., 1961.

White, Leslie A., "The Individual and the Culture Process" in *Centennial.* Washington, D.C.: American Association for the Advancement of Science, 1950.

Willey, Gordon R., *Prehistoric Settlement Patterns in the Virú Valley, Peru.* Bureau of American Ethnology, Bulletin 155. Washington, D.C.: Smithsonian Institution, 1953.

———, "The Prehistoric Civilizations of Nuclear America," *American Anthropologist,* LVII (1955), 571-93.

———, "The Early Great Styles and the Rise of the Pre-Columbian Civilizations," *American Anthropologist,* LXIV (1962), 1-14.

Wittfogel, Karl A., *Wirtschaft und Gesellschaft Chinas. Erster Teil. Produktivkräfte, Produktions- und Zirkulationsprozess.* Leipzig: C. L. Hirschfeld, 1931.

——, *Oriental Despotism: A Comparative Study of Total Power.* New Haven: Yale University Press, 1957.

Wolf, Eric R., "The Virgin of Guadalupe: A Mexican National Symbol," *Journal of American Folklore,* LXXI (1958), 34-39.

Zingg, Robert M., "The Genuine and Spurious Values in Tarahumara Culture," *American Anthropologist,* XLIV (1942), 78-92.

INDEX